The Young Nation:
America 1787-1861

Volume 5

SLAVERY AND THE COMING STORM

David M. Brownstone
Irene M. Franck

GROLIER
EDUCATIONAL

About This Book

The Young Nation explores the history of the United States from the Constitution to the Civil War in 10 volumes. The first five volumes are roughly chronological, with Vol. 1 taking up American beginnings and Vol. 5 focusing strongly on slavery. The last five volumes are thematic (see the back cover for the titles).

The text of this work is supplemented throughout by boxes, sidebars, chronologies, and more than 800 full-color images, including historical paintings and photographs, plus many maps, charts, and tables specially created for this set.

Each volume includes a Master Index to the whole set. In addition, frequent cross-references in place refer readers to related sections elsewhere in the set.

Each volume also includes bibliographies of Internet sites and books for those who wish to explore that volume's topics further. More general bibliographies of Internet sites and books are provided in Vol. 10.

Also in Vol. 10 are some special materials for the period covered by the set, including:
- a table of population growth by state and territory, including breakdowns by race and by rural or urban residence;
- a list of the Presidents, including inauguration date, party, and key opponent;
- the full text of the U.S. Constitution and its first 12 Amendments;
- a Words to Know section, defining and explaining key words and concepts (which are also explained in place in the text).

Published 2002 by Grolier Educational
Old Sherman Turnpike
Danbury, Connecticut 06816

Illustration credits for all 10 volumes of *The Young Nation* are given on pp. 87–88 of Vol. 10.

Library of Congress Cataloging-in-Publication Data

Brownstone, David M.
     The young nation : America 1787-1861 / David M. Brownstone, Irene M. Franck.
        p. cm.
     Includes bibliographic references and index.
     Contents: v. 1. A new nation — v. 2. The early years — v. 3. The way West — v. 4. Beyond the Mississippi — v. 5. Slavery and the coming storm — v. 6. The new Americans — v. 7. Women's lives, women's rights — v. 8. Science, technology, and everyday life — v. 9. The arts, literature, religion, and education — v. 10. A growing nation.
     ISBN 0-7172-5645-6 (hard : set : alk. paper). —ISBN 0-7172-5646-4 (hard : v. 1 : alk. paper). —
ISBN 0-7172-5647-2 (hard : v. 2 : alk. paper). —ISBN 0-7172-5648-0 (hard : v. 3 : alk. paper). —
ISBN 0-7172-5649-9 (hard : v. 4 : alk. paper). —ISBN 0-7172-5650-2 (hard : v. 5 : alk. paper). —
ISBN 0-7172-5651-0 (hard : v. 6 : alk. paper). —ISBN 0-7172-5652-9 (hard : v. 7 : alk. paper). —
ISBN 0-7172-5653-7 (hard : v. 8 : alk. paper). —ISBN 0-7172-5654-5 (hard : v. 9 : alk. paper). —
ISBN 0-7172-5655-3 (hard : v. 10 : alk. paper).
     1. United States—History—1783-1865—Juvenile literature. [1. United States—History—1783-1865.] 1. Franck, Irene M. II. Title.

E301 .B76 2002
973—dc21   2002020047

Printed in the United States of America
Designed by K & P Publishing Services

Contents

SLAVERY IN THE NEW
UNITED STATES   5

The Continuing Slave Trade   7
Outlawing the International Slave
    Trade   10
The Internal Slave Trade   12
The Growth of American Slavery   16
Free African Americans   19
Early African-American Resistance 22
American Slave Revolts   25
    The Amistad Mutiny   28
The Abolitionists   29
The Underground Railroad   32

THE ROAD TO SECESSION
AND WAR   36

The Election of 1848   39
    Zachary Taylor   40
    Millard Fillmore   40
The Compromise of 1850   42
    The Nashville Convention   43
Resisting the Fugitive Slave Act 45
Uncle Tom's Cabin   48
The Southern View of Slavery   50
The Election of 1852   52
    Franklin Pierce   53
The Opening of Japan   54

Filibusters South   56
  The Gadsden Purchase   57
The Kansas-Nebraska Act   58
The Transcontinental Routes   60

THE RESHAPING OF
AMERICAN POLITICS   64

The Know-Nothings   65
The Republican Party   68
Bleeding Kansas   70
The Buchanan Presidency   73
  James Buchanan   74
The Dred Scott Decision   75
The Lincoln-Douglas Debates   77
Harpers Ferry   80
The Election of 1860   83
  Abraham Lincoln   84
Secession and War   87

On the Internet   88
In Print   88
Master Index   89

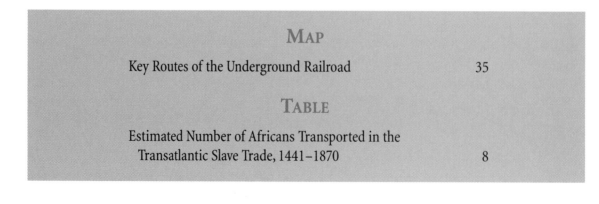

MAP
Key Routes of the Underground Railroad   35

TABLE
Estimated Number of Africans Transported in the
Transatlantic Slave Trade, 1441–1870   8

Slavery was part of the new United States from the beginning. This is a picture of George Washington (on horseback) and his family at their home, Mount Vernon, with some of their slaves.

Slavery in the New United States

By the 1790s—when the new United States was beginning its life as a unified, independent nation—slavery was a long-established institution throughout the country. Slavery was losing ground in the North but gaining ground in the South. It would soon experience tremendous growth in the South, with the invention of the cotton gin and the great push west in the Deep South.

At the same time, slavery was a deep, bitter issue. Together with the question of secession (see Vol. 3, p. 67), it would—after a series of compromises—deeply divide and finally tear apart the American nation, in the end leading to the Civil War. The long conflict over slavery, deferred during the adoption of the Constitution (see Vol. 1, p. 63), began again in the 1790s. It would soon grow into a major national issue.

The Union survived its first secession and slavery crisis in 1820 with the Missouri Compromise (see Vol. 3, p. 58) and its second slavery and secession crisis with the Compromise of 1850 (see p. 42).

After that, however, the final crisis would come on quickly and powerfully. The Fugitive Slave Act, the Kansas-Nebraska Act, the formation of the antislavery Republican Party, the growth of the southern secession movement, "Bleeding Kansas," the Dred Scott decision, John Brown at Harpers Ferry, and the election of Abraham Lincoln were all milestones on the road to secession, the Civil War, and the end of slavery.

The slave trade was international. A Dutch ship brought 20 slaves to Jamestown, Virginia, in 1619, the first introduction of Black Africans into what would become the United States.

This scene in the hold of the "Blood-Stained Gloria" is an engraving from Philip Drake's Revelations of a Slave Smuggler *(1858).*

The Continuing Slave Trade

Long before there was a United States, slavery was a large presence on the American scene. In 1619 the first 20 Black Africans were brought to Jamestown, Virginia. These were the first African Americans. From 1619 until Union victory in the Civil War, 246 years later, an estimated 400,000 to 500,000 African men, women, and children were shipped to what became the United States to be sold as slaves. Some had been kidnapped in Africa and were sent directly to American slave markets.

Others had been sent as slaves first to the Caribbean and later to the mainland. Still others were the children of people who had been born slaves elsewhere in the Americas and then shipped to the United States for sale in slave markets.

Though an enormous number, African slaves shipped to the United States were only a small fraction of those Africans who were captured and sold into slavery in the Atlantic slave trade. Between 1441, when the Portuguese began the Atlantic slave

Estimated Number of Africans Transported in the Transatlantic Slave Trade, 1441–1870

Destination	Estimated Number Transported
Brazil	3,500,000–4,000,000
Caribbean	3,800,000–4,300,000
Spanish Americas (except Caribbean)	1,550,000–1,750,000
Europe and Atlantic Islands	275,000–325,000
United States and Earlier Colonies	400,000–500,000
Other	75,000–625,000
Total	9,600,000–11,500,000

Note: At least 2 million more did not survive the journey.

TO BE SOLD, on board the Ship *Bance-Ifland*, on tuefday the 6th of May next, at *Afhley-Ferry*, a choice cargo of about 250 fine healthy NEGROES, juft arrived from the Windward & Rice Coaft. —The utmoft care has already been taken, and fhall be continued, to keep them free from the leaft danger of being infected with the SMALL-POX, no boat having been on board, and all other communication with people from *Charles-Town* prevented. *Auftin*, *Laurens*, & *Appleby*.

N. B. Full one Half of the above Negroes have had the SMALL-POX in their own Country.

Largely because of terrible conditions on board slave ships, African captives were prey to many diseases. Americans also feared that such diseases would be spread to them, so slave traders attempted to reassure potential buyers that their slaves were free of diseases, such as the smallpox mentioned in this poster.

trade, and 1870, when it was finally ended, an estimated 11.4 to 13.8 million Africans were taken out of Africa against their will, transported in the Atlantic slave trade, and sold as slaves. Of these, at least 2 million did not survive the journey. Of the estimated 9.6 million to 11.5 million who did survive, a little less than 5 percent went to Britain's North American colonies and later to the United States.

Conditions on the slave ships were crowded, unhealthy, and brutal. They were the direct cause of the millions of deaths that occurred, in what many—with complete justification—have called another kind of Holocaust. No one is able to estimate how many more Africans arrived so weakened and sick after their terrible journeys that they did not long survive, but the number was enormous.

Uncounted numbers also fell ill and died afterward when they were exposed to epidemic diseases for which their bodies had developed no resistance. In this, many shared the fate of the millions of Native Americans who died of epidemic diseases brought by Europeans to the Americas.

Beyond that, the work, especially on the sugar plantations of the Caribbean, was literally killing. Meanwhile, planta-

Now that the whole ship's cargo were confined together, it became absolutely pestilential. The closeness of the place, and the heat of the climate . . . almost suffocated us. . . . The shrieks of the women, and the groans of the dying rendered it a scene of horror almost inconceivable. . . . I began to hope that death would soon put an end to my miseries.

OLAUDAH EQUIANO, ENSLAVED IN AFRICA AT AGE 12 AND BROUGHT TO THE AMERICAS

tion owners reaped large profits from the unpaid labor of slaves who were forced to work as much as 18 to 20 hours a day—as long as they lived.

In the slave markets of what became the United States, Africans who had survived their terrible journeys were sold by slave traders to American slaveholders. They were sold for their entire lives. Children born in slavery became the property of the slaveholders who owned their mothers. Even when parents and children arrived together on the slave ships, they were often separately, most of them never to see each other again.

Seeking to escape, some kidnapped Africans leaped off the ships meant to carry them into slavery. To prevent that, slave traders put most captives in chains and shackles—metal circlets, usually paired, linking their wrists or ankles.

This sailing ship looks beautiful and perhaps even romantic, but it was used to transport Africans by the hundreds into slavery in the Americas. After the abolition of the international slave trade in 1807, the British actively boarded possible slave ships to stop the trade. Americans enforced the law less actively.

Outlawing the International Slave Trade

In the mid-1700s some people called for outlawing the slave trade, especially Quakers in Britain and its American colonies. Yet the slave trade continued and grew, for it was enormously profitable. A single slave ship voyage often yielded profits of two or three times the cost of the ship itself, with ship-owners and captains quickly becoming rich from their murderous trade.

Despite the resistance of slave traders and slaveholders, the movement to outlaw the international slave trade grew very strong in Britain and the United States in the late 1700s. It began to win major victories in the early 1800s. Britain and the United States outlawed the international slave trade in 1807. Many European nations soon followed suit.

Although formally outlawed, the Atlantic slave trade continued—just not as freely as before. In U.S. courts the new laws were seldom strongly enforced. Slave ships stopped by the U.S. Navy were often soon freed to pursue their trade again.

British warships far more actively enforced the ban on the slave trade. However, they could not legally board American merchant ships carrying slaves. The situation changed somewhat as the United States, Britain, and other nations made agreements that allowed their navies to jointly board ships suspected of carrying slaves.

Yet enforcement was still far from effective. Some slaves were smuggled into the United States even past the beginning of the Civil War. Slave smuggling was stopped only when the Union navy blockaded the southern coastline during that war.

Estimates vary widely, but some 50,000 to 60,000 slaves were probably smuggled into the United States between 1807, when the slave trade was outlawed, and the early 1860s, when it was finally stopped.

This is the deck of the slave ship Wildfire, *bringing slaves to Key West, Florida, in 1860—more than 50 years after the slave trade had supposedly been banned by the United States.*

New Orleans was a major center in the internal slave trade of the United States. This is a sale of "estates, pictures, and slaves" in a rotunda (high-domed room) in New Orleans in the 1840s.

The Internal Slave Trade

A second kind of slave trade existed within the United States. That was the business of selling and reselling enslaved African Americans within the country.

From the start many enslaved African Americans in the United States were bought and sold more than once in their lifetimes. That often happened when a slaveowner died or fell on hard times and was forced to sell properties—including human beings. At such times, African-American families were often broken up and their lives uprooted. The buyers of such slaves were often planters and farmers who were expanding their landholdings.

The internal American slave trade changed and massively expanded in the early 1800s, as the main focus of slavery in the South turned to the "Black Belt" states of the Deep South—Georgia, Mississippi, Alabama, and Louisiana. Several major factors caused the change:

- By the early 1800s plantation farmlands in the Old South—Virginia, Maryland, and the Carolinas—had been overcultivated to produce just a few cash crops, most notably tobacco. Many planters in the Old South were in the process of going broke and had far more slaves than they needed to work their failing land.

- In 1793 Eli Whitney invented the cotton gin (see Vol. 10, p. 33). This made it possible to remove cotton seeds by machine, rather than by hand. That, in turn, made it possible to produce cotton far more cheaply than before. However, large numbers of workers were still needed to cultivate and pick the cotton. In the South these workers were slaves. The emergence of cotton as the South's major cash-producing crop changed the region's economy tremendously.

- In the early 1800s southern cotton planters began a powerful push west, seizing richly productive Native-American lands in the Black Belt, legally or illegally (see Vol. 3, p. 39). There they built what came to be called the Cotton Kingdom. Al-

The expansion of cotton cultivation into the Deep South and the invention of the cotton gin led to greatly increased demand for slaves to work in the cotton fields, hoeing and picking the cotton, as here on the Mississippi River.

To keep them from escaping, slaves were chained together in a line called a coffle, like this one being led by a man on horseback. Sometimes they were walked that way for hundreds of miles to be sold at auction.

though many planters brought slaves with them, they needed many more slaves to work their new lands.

- In 1807 the importing of slaves was outlawed. Many slaves were still smuggled into the South (see p. 11). However, the planters of the Cotton Kingdom needed far more slaves than could be brought in from abroad.

The net effect of these factors was to create a large and highly profitable new business in the South—the expanded internal slave trade. Slave traders bought slaves in the Old South and transported them to the Cotton Kingdom states of the Deep South.

In the process they established a web of holding pens, jails, and means of transport for the hundreds of thousands of slaves they sold. Some slaves were sent by sea south along the Atlantic coast and the Gulf of Mexico, often to New Orleans. Others were walked in chained caravans, just as kidnapped slaves had been walked out of Africa to the slave ports on the African coast. Some slaves walked part of the way and were then shipped south on the Mississippi River.

All of the main cities of the Old South were slave shipment points. Washington, D.C., the capital of the United States, was one of the main centers of the trade in enslaved African Americans. That ended only after the slave trade was outlawed there as part of the Compromise of 1850 (see p. 42).

(see p. 42)

This tremendous expansion of the domestic slave trade caused African-American family breakups on a massive scale—though many people in the South denied that such breakups occurred. Another result was the widespread practice of "breeding" new slaves. Also much denied, this practice used African-American mothers to give birth. The sons and daughters—while still children—would then be separated from their mothers and sold at great profit into slavery in the Deep South. Most parents and children, or husbands and wives, separated by the slave trade never saw each other again.

This (at left) is a copy of an invoice for a sale of African-American slaves in 1835. John W. Pittman sold 10 slaves for a total of $5,254.50, to which he added his expenses of another $96.50. His note at the bottom reads: "I did intend to leave Nancy['s] child but she made such a damned fuss I had to let her take it. I could of got fifty Dollars for [it] so you must add forty Dollars to the above." Such a slave mother's anguish is shown below.

Not all slaves worked on huge plantations. Some lived and worked on farms owned by only modestly prosperous Southerners, as here on the Pascagoula River in Mississippi in the early 1800s.

The Growth of American Slavery

The numbers of slaves grew very fast from 1790 to 1860, as did the number of free African Americans. The first U.S. census, in 1790, showed an estimated African-American population of a little over 757,000. Of these, 698,000 were slaves and 59,000 free African Americans.

Only 30 years later, in 1820, the African-American population had more than doubled to over 1,870,000 African Americans—1,538,000 slaves and 333,000 free African Americans. That was more than twice as many slaves and more than five times as many free African Americans as in 1790.

By 1860, approaching the Civil War, there were 4,440,000 African Americans. Almost 4 million of these were slaves and 488,000 free. In only 70 years there were more than six times as many slaves as in 1790, and more than eight times as many free African Americans.

Boston was a center of antislavery activity. Here Wendell Phillips spoke in 1851 at an antislavery meeting on Boston Common, to an audience of men and women, both Whites and African Americans.

A relatively small number of big plantation owners, with large numbers of slaves, dominated southern life. Only one out of four Southerners held slaves, and most of them held fewer than four slaves.

Yet cotton was the region's great cash crop, and the big planters held the keys to widespread prosperity or failure throughout the South. Beyond that, Southerners were united by common fears. They made the South into an armed camp, full of local slave patrols. State militias were always on alert for slave revolts, whether or not they happened. As sentiment against slavery strengthened in the North, and highly pub-licized slave revolts began to occur in the South (see p. 25), fears of slave revolt grew to fever pitch.

Slave Codes

A whole second system of laws, called the Black Codes, or Slave Codes, grew up in the colonial period. It was not limited to the South. For example, New York adopted repressive slave codes in 1702. Virginia, which already had many repressive slave laws, turned its large body of laws into a single slave code in 1705. As slavery was abolished in the North, these slave codes were ended there. However, they grew into

17

a massive body of repressive laws in the South during the 1800s.

The slave codes were aimed at completely controlling slaves and stopping slave

> *None can feel the lash but those who have it upon them . . . none know where the chain galls but those who wear it.*
>
> THEODORE S. WRIGHT, THE FIRST AFRICAN AMERICAN TO GRADU-ATE FROM AN AMERICAN THEOLOGICAL SEMINARY, PASTOR OF THE FIRST COLORED PRESBYTERIAN CHURCH IN NEW YORK CITY, AND A FOUNDER OF THE NEW YORK ANTI-SLAVERY SOCIETY.

revolts before they could get started. They provided very harsh punishments for a wide range of matters, some of them very small, such as visiting a free African American. Punishments ranged from whipping to branding, mutilation, and death.

Slaves were very often punished with little or no proof that they had actually violated the slave laws. Slaves had none of the rights and protections of Whites before the law. They could not even defend themselves in court, for they could not sue others or testify against a White person.

The aim of the slave codes was to establish a system in which African Americans were treated as property, rather than human beings, and to control slaves by suppressing any sign of possible revolt. In practice, the slave codes established an increasingly harsh system of terror in the South during the 1800s, as slaveholders felt more and more threatened by slave resistance and antislavery Northerners (see p. 25).

The everyday life of slaves is part of the wider picture of life in the early United States, covered in several other volumes. See the Master Index at the end of each volume for references.

Slaves could be whipped, and often with extreme brutality, at the will of the slave owner or the overseer. This scene is based on an eyewitness's account of such a whipping, from a book by a Boston woman teaching in Virginia before the Civil War.

Free African Americans

Born in slavery in 1817, Frederick Douglass escaped in 1838 to become a leading speaker, writer, and organizer for the abolitionist cause, as well as for women's rights and several other social reforms. This portrait, probably painted by Elisha Hammond, shows him in 1844. Douglass became a national figure with publication of his autobiography, Narrative of the Life of Frederick Douglass, an American Slave (1845). Founder of the antislavery publication The North Star (1847), he organized African-American troops during the Civil War. After the war he held several government positions, including that of Minister to Haiti (1889–1891).

Many free African Americans played important roles as the crisis over slavery developed. Free African Americans in the South were increasingly restricted as fear of slave resistance grew to panic proportions (see p. 25). However, many in the North were active abolitionists (see p. 29). Free African Americans were also active in founding religious and educational institutions (see Vol. 9, pp. 18 and 85).

Small numbers of free African Americans came to the United States before the Civil War. Often they came from countries in which slavery had been abolished, among them Haiti.

However, the vast majority of free African Americans arrived as slaves but later won or were granted their freedom.

> *What, to the American slave, is your Fourth of July? I answer: A day that reveals to him, more than all other days of the year, the gross injustice and cruelty to which he is the constant victim. To him your celebration is a sham. . . .*
>
> *You profess to believe that "of one blood God made all nations of men to dwell on the face of all the earth"—and hath commanded all men, everywhere, to love one another—yet you notoriously hate (and glory in your hatred!) all men whose skins are not colored like your own!*
>
> FREDERICK DOUGLASS, IN A SPEECH AT ROCHESTER, NEW YORK, JULY 4, 1852

The children of free African-American mothers were born free—though many who were born free were enslaved in the South during their lifetimes. For example, many free African Americans were accused of being escaped slaves and were then enslaved, for they had very little ability to defend themselves before the law.

Slaves could become free in several ways. Many in the North were freed when slavery was abolished in their states. Others, North and South, were freed by the

This 1880s image honors "Heroes of the Colored Race." Among the key figures are some from before the Civil War, including Frederick Douglass (center, flanked by Blanche Kelso Bruce and Hiram Rhoades Revels) and John Brown (bottom center).

Many free African Americans ran their own small businesses, especially in the North, often serving other African Americans, as here.

wills of their late slaveowners or by those who had inherited them as slaves. Sometimes those freed were the children of White male slaveowners and enslaved African-American women.

Quite large numbers of slaves bought their freedom. They earned enough money to do so by working for hire, which they could legally do with the agreement of their owners. As the North-South split over slavery grew, along with southern dread of slave revolts, some southern states barred slaves from buying their freedom.

Free African Americans were banned from many trades and professions in both North and South. Most worked as laborers on farms and in the cities. However, sub-

stantial numbers were able to learn skills and make their living in a wide range of higher-paying occupations.

Most free African Americans worked for others. However, many were able to build their own small businesses, as tailors, carpenters, masons, shopkeepers, and other such occupations.

Few free African Americans became wealthy, but a good many prospered. In the South, some—but only a few—even held slaves. Prosperous or poor, however, free African Americans shared a common commitment to educate their children. This was especially so because some southern states barred teaching slaves how to read (see Vol. 9, p. 12).

Over the years many African Americans fled from slavery into the swamps, as these escapees did in the early years of the Civil War.

Early African-American Resistance

From the earliest days of American slavery, slave resistance was expressed in many ways. Most commonly, slaves simply ran away from slavery. That is what tens of thousands of southern slaves did. Many found their way north to freedom in the 1800s, often with the help of the Underground Railroad (see p. 32).

Others fleeing slavery became Maroons (a Spanish and French term for fugitive slaves). Whether in Jamaica or the lower Mississippi Valley, in Haiti or in Spanish Florida, Maroons were former slaves. They had fled into the back country of their island or region, or into nonslave territories, and established free communities of their own, often raiding back into slave territories.

In Jamaica and Haiti, for example, large Maroon communities successfully fought

22

Escaped slaves were often chased by hunters with guns and dogs, like the ones that have treed this fugitive.

French, Spanish, and British forces for two centuries, until the European powers gave up and left them alone. In the United States smaller, but well-established Maroon communities existed in Florida, Virginia's Great Dismal Swamp, the lower Mississippi Valley, and the Chesapeake Bay region. Florida's Maroons fought beside the Creeks and Seminoles in the early 1800s (see Vol. 3, p. 40).

Large numbers of American slaves did not flee at all. Instead, they stayed on as slaves, doing their work with as little cooperation as possible and often sabotaging tools and crops. A few became free (see p. 19). Some slaves—the most greatly feared of all—resisted slavery by organizing and joining slave uprisings.

Throughout the history of American slavery, slaveholders greatly feared rebellions—and for excellent reasons. Scores of African-American uprisings occurred on slave ships crossing the Atlantic. At least hundreds and probably thousands more slave uprisings occurred throughout the South, though most of them have not been recorded. There were also uprisings of enslaved Native Americans, as in the Spanish Southwest and California.

The Haitian Slave Revolt

The largest, the most deadly by far, and the most menacing of all slave uprisings did not take place in the United States but in Haiti. In 1791 François-Dominique Toussaint (later L'Ouverture) led a huge slave rebellion on French-held Haiti on the

23

island of Santo Domingo (then Saint-Dominique). At the same time a smaller uprising began on the island, of free African Haitians and mulattos (people of more than one racial background).

L'Ouverture's forces, numbering an estimated 100,000, besieged Haiti's capital, Port-au-Prince, in 1792. However, after France abolished slavery, they pulled back and joined the French in their war against Britain. Tens of thousands of African Haitians and thousands of French died in the war, including thousands of the island's French settlers. During and after the war thousands of White Haitians and many free African Haitians fled to the United States, most of them to New Orleans but some to other southern port cities.

In the years that followed, L'Ouverture's Haitian forces and the French fought and defeated the British in Haiti. In 1799 L'Ouverture's forces also defeated and destroyed the free Haitian Black and mu-latto republic that had been established in southern Haiti.

The French turned on their Haitian allies in 1801, sending a force of 22,000 French troops to reconquer Haiti and to reestablish slavery on the island. In 1802 the French took L'Ouverture while he was negotiating peace with them; he died in prison in 1803.

However, the French could not conquer Haiti. Until late 1803 they fought a failed, bitter war that cost thousands more lives on both sides, many of them executed civilians and prisoners of war.

In 1804 L'Ouverture's successor, John-Jacques Dessalines, ordered the massacre of every White left on the island. Though some escaped, most were killed.

In the American South, Whites afraid of massive slave revolts remembered well the Haitian wars and massacres—and so did African-American slaves.

Toussaint L'Ouverture led the violent and very successful slave rebellion in Haiti (on the island of Santo Domingo, then called Saint-Dominique).

This image, "Horrid Massacre in Virginia," appeared in the 1831 book **Authentic and Impartial Narrative of the Tragical Scene Which Was Witnessed in Southampton County,** *about the Nat Turner revolt. It triggered great fear about possible further slave rebellions.*

American Slave Revolts

American slavery also produced revolts, though none remotely like the huge Haitian uprisings and wars. Some of the earliest reported slave revolts were not in the South but in the colony of New York in 1708 and 1712. In 1741 New York also had more than 30 executions, of African-American slaves and some Whites accused of plotting a slave revolt, even though no revolt had taken place.

Two substantial slave revolts did take place in and near Charleston, South Carolina, in September 1739. Both of these in-volved groups of slaves trying to fight their way to freedom in Spanish-held St. Augustine, Florida. One group killed 21 Whites before they were stopped and themselves killed. The second group, heading for Florida, killed a reported 30 Whites before they were stopped; they were later executed.

A much larger slave revolt, planned along the lines of the Haitian Revolution, was organized by slave Gabriel Prosser in Henrico County, Virginia, in August 1800. In some ways it might have been a model for John Brown's attack on Harpers Ferry

Many slave revolts in the United States took their model from Haiti. This is Nat Turner and others planning their revolt in 1831.

59 years later. Prosser organized an army of 1,100 slaves, crudely armed and with few guns. He planned to lead his army in an attack on Richmond, Virginia, expecting that he would trigger a huge slave uprising and form a new, free government.

Whether that would have worked out as he expected will never be known, for he was betrayed by some of his own people. The revolt was crushed before it could get started. He, his family, and 24 other slaves were later executed—but fear of a massive slave uprising swept the South.

Of the many slave revolts in the decade that followed, probably the most notable was that of an estimated 500 slaves near New Orleans, Louisiana, in January 1811.

Led by Charles Deslandes, the rebels destroyed several plantations in the area before they were taken. Many of the rebels were later executed.

Denmark Vesey

In the spring of 1822 Haiti-born former slave Denmark Vesey, a free African American, organized a massive slave revolt at Charleston, South Carolina. His plan, like that of Gabriel Prosser 22 years earlier, used the model provided by the Haitian Revolution. Vesey, with other free and enslaved African Americans, organized an estimated 7,000 to 9,000 slaves in the Charleston area into a slave army. Their plan was to rise in late July, take Charleston and any stores of weapons available there, and massacre all the Whites in and around Charleston. Vesey believed that the rebellion would spread like wildfire throughout the South, and that Haiti and Britain would quickly move to the aid of the revolution.

Like Prosser, Vesey was betrayed by some of his own people. The planned revolt was stopped before it began. Vesey and 34 others were executed.

In the wake of the failed revolt, as a new wave of fear swept the South, even more repressive Black Codes were adopted in South Carolina. Many of the new laws were aimed at free African Americans, as well as slaves (see p. 17).

Nat Turner's Revolt

On August 21, 1831, in Southampton County, Virginia, enslaved African-American minister Nat Turner organized and carried through a slave revolt and accompanying massacre. Turner's force of 70 slaves killed 60 Whites in the course of the two-day rebellion. That ended when the slaves were attacked and taken by federal troops, with many rebels dead. Turner fled but was later captured and executed, as were 20 other captured rebels.

Turner had hoped the rising would turn into a wide-scale revolution. Although it did not spread, it caused a tremendous

Though he initially escaped, Nat Turner was hunted, captured, and later executed. His 1831 revolt caused great fear to spread in the South, triggering passage of harshly repressive laws against all African Americans, slave and free.

alarm throughout the South. It also led to further hardening of repressive laws.

Turner's revolt had come only eight months after William Lloyd Garrison's call for action to abolish slavery in the first issue of *The Liberator* (see p. 30). It also helped trigger southern fears of northern abolitionists. Southerners thought that these abolitionists were out to destroy the South and slavery by organizing murderous slave revolts. Along with new, much harsher Black Codes (see p. 17), many southern states passed new laws aimed at abolitionism and abolitionist literature. Garrison himself became a wanted man in many parts of the South.

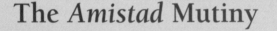

The *Amistad* Mutiny

This picture shows kidnapped Africans killing the captain of the slave ship Amistad, as they sought to escape slavery. It appeared in an 1840 book called History of the Amistad Captives.

The *Amistad* mutiny was a different kind of slave revolt. This one brought a former president of the United States before the U.S. Supreme Court. It ended with the freeing of the mutineers and generated a surge of antislavery sentiment in the North.

The *Amistad* was a Spanish ship being used to transport 53 newly arrived African slaves from Havana, Cuba, to Cuban coastal plantations. In July 1839, 53 slaves, led by Joseph Cinque, took control of the ship. They killed the captain and some of the crew, and then forced other crew members to sail the ship toward Sierra Leone, Africa. However, the crew fooled the mutineers as to where they were going, sailing instead into Montauk, Long Island, where the mutineers were arrested.

Abolitionist Northerners challenged their arrest and began a lawsuit. Former U.S. president John Quincy Adams (see Vol. 3, p. 64) defended the mutineers before the U.S. Supreme Court and won their freedom. The case was highly publicized throughout the North, becoming a landmark antislavery victory.

Abolitionists were often the targets of violence, both verbal and physical. This is the printshop of abolitionist E. P. Lovejoy, in Alton, Illinois, which was burned in 1835.

The Abolitionists

The long campaign to abolish American slavery began during the colonial period, with the antislavery Quakers leading the way. In 1688 Pennsylvania Quakers passed the first known American resolution condemning slavery. That was followed by a long series of Quaker resolutions and actions aimed at abolishing slavery in the colonies. The Quakers were joined by other churches in the late 1700s, most notably by the Methodist Episcopal Church in the early 1780s. The first of many petitions to abolish slavery was sent to the U.S. Congress in 1790 (see Vol. 2, p. 5). One of them was presented by Benjamin Franklin,

the founding president of the Pennsylvania Abolition Society.

As the national argument over slavery intensified, abolitionism expanded to include a wide range of antislavery activists, far beyond the Quakers and other early opponents of slavery. Antislavery societies were formed in many states, and antislavery educational institutions, such as Maine's Bowdoin College (1794), were founded. Free African Americans also began to develop many antislavery organizations and institutions. By 1820, when the sharp argument over slavery in the territories resulted in the Missouri Compromise (see Vol. 3,

work had tremendous impact in both North and South.

In the 1830s the abolition movement emerged as an increasingly powerful force. It gathered more and more strength in communities throughout the North, as well as in state and national governments. In 1831 William Lloyd Garrison's *The Liberator* and Nat Turner's revolt also helped generate a strong abolitionist movement. Garrison was a founder of the New England Anti-Slavery Society in

p. 58), antislavery was firmly rooted, and abolitionism was on the verge of becoming a major national movement—though the idea was still widely resisted in the North, as well as hated and feared in the South.

In 1829 free African American David Walker published his powerful *Appeal to the Colored Peoples of the World*, calling on African Americans to fight for their freedom in the South, including slave revolts. His

I will be as harsh as truth and as uncompromising as justice. On this subject [slavery] I do not wish to think, or speak, or write, with moderation. No! No! Tell a man whose house is on fire to give a moderate alarm; tell him to moderately rescue his wife from the hands of the ravisher; tell the mother to gradually extricate her babe from the fire into which it has fallen; but urge me not to use moderation.

WILLIAM LLOYD GARRISON, IN *THE LIBERATOR*, NO. 1, JANUARY 1, 1831

As soon as their escape was discovered, slaves were hunted, often with dogs, as here. With little to guide them but their own ingenuity and hearsay tales of other escapes, they would often follow a watercourse as a road to freedom.

During all my slave life I never lost sight of freedom. It was always on my heart; it came to me like a solemn thought, and often circumstances much stimulated the desire to be free and raised great expectation of it. We slaves all knew when an Abolitionist got into Congress. We knew it when there was just one there, and we watched it all the way until there was a majority there.

AMBROSE HEADEN, BORN 1822,
A SLAVE IN NORTH CAROLINA AND ALABAMA

1831. On the national scene Theodore Weld and Arthur Tappan were among the founders of the American Anti-Slavery Society in 1833.

In the same period women began to form antislavery societies (see Vol. 7, p. 19). The first, founded by a group of free African-American women, was the Salem Anti-Slavery Society in Massachusetts in 1832.

In the 1840s Frederick Douglass and Harriet Tubman would emerge as the best-known African-American leaders of the abolition movement. He was that movement's most effective speaker. She was one of the most successful "conductors" in the Underground Railroad (see p. 32).

Levi Coffin was sometimes called the "President of the Underground Railroad." In Charles T. Webber's painting **The Underground Railroad,** *he and his wife, Catharine Coffin, are shown leading some fugitive African Americans to temporary shelter in their home in Indiana, before sending them on their way to safety farther north.*

The Underground Railroad

People who were against slavery—both African Americans and Whites—had been helping escaping slaves since long before the American Revolution. In the early 1800s that help took a far more organized form. Antislavery activists developed a set of escape routes and safe houses for fugitive slaves. Together these were called the Underground Railroad.

The Underground Railroad was not a single escape route out of the South. Instead, it was a large group of escape routes north, west, and south (see p. 35).

Many who fled to freedom stayed in the North. Often they worked under assumed names and lived in free African-American communities. Many others were helped to flee to Canada, the Caribbean, and Mexico.

Early in the 1800s many slaves fled to freedom in Spanish-held Florida and Texas (see Vol. 3, pp. 40 and 77). Later the great majority escaped to the North, "following the North Star." That was literally true, for escaping slaves traveled by night, often using the North Star as their guide. Part of the Little Dipper constellation, the North Star is pointed to by two stars in the Big Dipper. Escapees called that the "drinking gourd," celebrated in their song "Follow the Drinking Gourd" (see Vol. 9, p. 52).

The "stations" on the Underground Railroad were hundreds and perhaps thousands of homes and barns. There escaped slaves found shelter, food, clothing, medical help, and whatever else they needed to continue their journey to the next "station."

The thousands of abolitionists who helped escaping slaves were called "conductors." Some conductors, like Quaker Levi Coffin, helped thousands in their journeys to freedom. Some slaves were caught and returned to slavery, and many conductors were imprisoned because of their work, some for years.

Some conductors peacefully helped escaping slaves for many years. Others fought pitched battles against slave catchers to protect escaping slaves. An estimated

Many people, Blacks and Whites, helped operate the Underground Railroad. Some of them are shown here: Levi Coffin (top left), Josiah Henson (top right), David Ruggles (bottom left), and John and Jean Rankin.

Harriet Tubman escaped from slavery in 1849 and quickly became the most famous conductor on the Underground Railroad. Known as the "Moses" of the abolitionist movement, she returned to the slave states 19 times to lead more than 300 slaves to freedom, even though the South offered $40,000 for her capture. During the Civil War she was a scout, guerrilla fighter, spy, and nurse for the Union.

When I found I had crossed that line [on her first escape from slavery in 1845], I looked at my hands to see if I was the same person. There was such a glory over everything.

HARRIET TUBMAN, TO HER BIOGRAPHER SARAH H. BRADFORD, 1868

2,500 to 3,000 conductors worked in the Underground Railroad at its peak, with probably half of them in Ohio.

The chief escape routes on the Underground Railroad led out of the Cotton Kingdom states of Georgia, Alabama, Mississippi, and Louisiana. They went north into Ohio, Indiana, and Illinois, and from there into Canada.

A second major set of escape routes led out of the Carolinas and Virginia through Pennsylvania and New York to Canada. An alternate route went farther north through New England to Canada.

A third and smaller set of routes went north by sea along the Atlantic coast, to New York and Boston and from there by land to Canada. A smaller route went south through Florida and then by sea to the Caribbean. An even smaller, very difficult route went through Texas to Mexico, with escaping slaves sometimes being aided by Native Americans.

From the 1820s to the beginning of the Civil War, an estimated 100,000 slaves escaped to freedom with the help of the Underground Railroad.

> *I's hoping and praying all the time I meets up with that Harriet Tubman woman. She the colored woman what takes slaves to Canada. She always travels the underground railroad, they calls it, travels at night and hides out in the day. She sure sneaks them out the South, and I thinks she's a brave woman.*
>
> THOMAS COLE, BORN IN 1845, A FORMER SLAVE IN ALABAMA

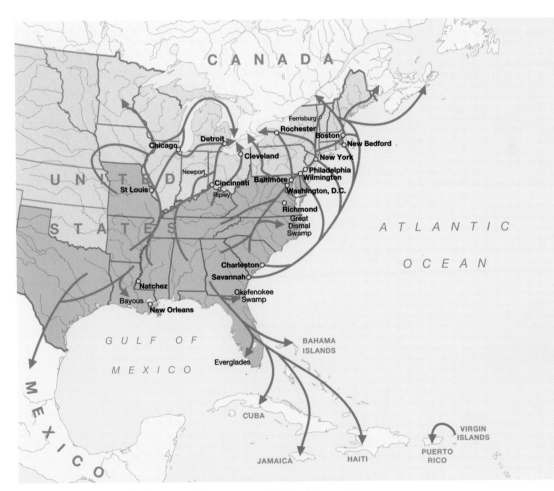

Key Routes of the Underground Railroad

The Road to Secession and War

The Mexican-American War and the Oregon Treaty took the United States to the Pacific (see Vol. 4, pp. 18 and 25). However, that only worsened the developing crisis over slavery and secession that would soon lead to the Civil War.

There was no great surge of unifying national pride in the United States after the victorious Mexican-American War; far from it. After the war many in the North became convinced all over again that the South had fought the war to gain more slave states. At the same time, many in the South believed that the North had been enormously strengthened by the acquisition of huge territories that would be settled by antislavery Northerners, who would create many more free states.

That is, in fact, what happened. The great mass of emigrants moved west to California and Oregon through the northern and central plains and mountains (see Vol. 4, p. 35), which had been part of the United States since the Louisiana Purchase. That meant that most of the new prairie and mountain states would be settled by Northerners and become free states.

Looking at a map of the United States as it was in 1849, anyone could clearly see that the North would become far more powerful relative to the South in the years and decades to come. However, many Southerners thought that upsetting the Missouri Compromise of 1820 (see Vol. 3, p. 58) might make the South able to swing some existing free states and some new states toward slavery. Proslavery forces in Congress, the states, and the Supreme Court then made a powerful and at first partially successful attack on the Missouri Compromise. Antislavery forces soon responded.

Much sharper conflicts over slavery quickly began, fed by the national political situation. During the run-up to the Civil War, the Democratic Party had large majorities in Congress, and Southerners controlled the Supreme Court. Both major parties, the Whigs and the Democrats, were coalition parties with northern and southern wings. However, by 1860 the Whigs had fragmented and were gone from the national political scene. The Democrats remained, and only on the eve of war would their northern and southern wings split over secession. That historic split would give the Presidency to Abraham Lincoln and the Republican Party in 1860.

In the late 1840s and through the 1850s, the country fell into crisis after worsening crisis. In those years the Fugitive Slave Act (1850), *Uncle Tom's Cabin* (1852), the Dred Scott decision (1857), and the growing Underground Railroad (see p. 32) would together with many similar events give the moral "high ground" to the antislavery North. That would cost the South dearly.

The Dred Scott decision also did much more than that, for it nullified the Missouri Compromise of 1820. That was part of the South's attempt to reopen the question of slavery in many free states, something the North would not do.

In the same period the Compromise of 1850, the Kansas-Nebraska Act (1854), the armed conflict between proslavery and antislavery forces in "Bloody Kansas," John Brown's raid (1859), and many other growing conflicts led directly to secession and the Civil War.

As emigrants continued to pour westward, like this wagon train in the Rocky Mountains of Colorado, the country began to reconsider the question of whether the new states and territories would be slave or free.

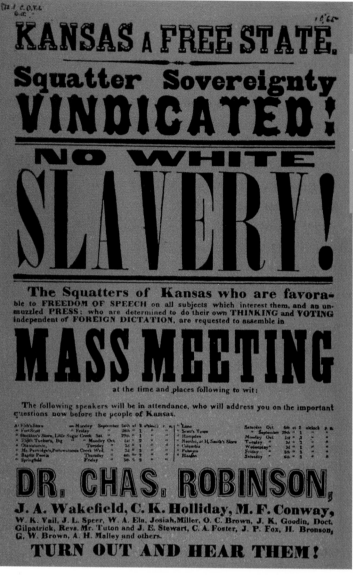

In the election of 1848, the idea of state sovereignty became a major issue. Also called "squatter sovereignty," as in this Kansas poster, this meant that a state could choose for itself whether to be slave or free, regardless of the Missouri Compromise of 1820.

The Election of 1848

In the presidential election of 1848, both major parties, the Whigs and the Democrats, tried very hard to avoid the question of slavery, by far the most important issue then facing the nation.

The Whigs succeeded. Their candidate was Mexican-American War hero Zachary Taylor, who had commanded American forces at Buena Vista (see Vol. 4, p. 26). Relying on his status as a war hero—and on the fact that he was a conservative Loui-siana slaveholder who would reassure southern voters—Taylor took no public position on slavery during the campaign. He went much further than that and ran on no platform at all. Instead, he promised to take no side in the slavery argument and to try to bring the two sides together.

The Democratic candidate was Senator Lewis Cass of Michigan. He did not avoid discussing slavery but took what he thought to be a compromise position. He called for

Zachary Taylor

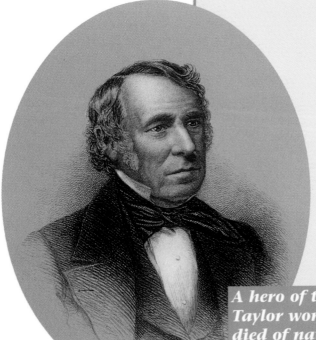

Zachary Taylor (1784–1850) was the 12th President of the United States (1849–1850). A minister and career soldier, he became a national figure during the Mexican-American War.

Born in Orange County, Virginia, Taylor had little formal education. He began his long military career in 1806, became a lieutenant in 1808, and served

A hero of the Mexican-American War, Zachary Taylor won the U.S. Presidency in 1848, but he died of natural causes after only 16 months in office. This portrait, probably by James Reid Lambdin, was painted that year.

state sovereignty, also called "squatter sovereignty," meaning that each state could choose whether or not to have slavery. However, that position did not satisfy a good many normally Democratic voters in both North and South, who felt that the issue of slavery had to be dealt with on the national level.

Former president Martin Van Buren also ran for the Presidency, as the candidate of the new antislavery Free Soil Party. The party was so named because it demanded free homesteads for those who settled on government-owned land. Van Buren won no electoral votes, but he won enough votes in New York to split that state's Democratic vote. That threw New York to Taylor, who

Millard Fillmore

Millard Fillmore (1800–1874) was the 13th President of the United States (1850–1853). A lawyer and politician, Fillmore was elected Vice President in 1848, succeeding Zachary Taylor to the Presidency after Taylor's death in 1850.

Born in Cayuga County, New York, Fillmore served in the New York State Assembly (1816–1833) and the U.S.

in the War of 1812. Leaving the army as a captain after the war, he rejoined it as a major in 1816. He became a brigadier general during the Second Seminole War (1835–1843).

Taylor became a very popular major general during the Mexican-American War, though he felt that he had been bypassed and left on occupation duty in northern Mexico during the later stages of the war. In 1848 he was the victorious Whig candidate for the Presidency.

won the election with 163 electoral votes to 127 for Cass. Millard Fillmore was elected Vice President.

While President, Zachary Taylor sharply opposed secession. He just as sharply opposed Henry Clay's "Omnibus Bill" in the spring of 1850 (see p. 42). This attempted to reach a full-scale national compromise on the issue of slavery.

However, Taylor died in office because of illness on July 9, 1850, after only 16 months as President. He was succeeded by Vice President Millard Fillmore, who saw the matter of slavery differently, with enormous consequences for the future of the country.

Millard Fillmore became the second Vice President to succeed to the Presidency while in office, after Zachary Taylor died in 1850.

House of Representatives (1834–1835; 1837–1843). With Henry Clay's backing he was nominated for the Vice-Presidency in 1848. Not renominated for the Presidency in 1852, he was the unsuccessful presidential candidate of the Know-Nothing Party in 1856, then retired from politics.

Kentucky Senator Henry Clay was called the "Great Compromiser" because of his key roles in developing the Compromises of 1820 and 1850. Here he addressed the Senate in 1850.

The Compromise of 1850

In 1850 the national argument over slavery became a completely dominant issue. By then the states and the members of Congress were identifying themselves as northern and southern, antislavery or proslavery, with all other issues and parties losing interest when compared with the issues of slavery and secession.

In May 1850 Senator Henry Clay of Kentucky was the chief architect of an Omnibus Bill. This sought to wrap up all of the main outstanding disagreements in a single compromise that would satisfy everyone. President Zachary Taylor (see p. 40) sharply opposed the Omnibus Bill. Even after his death it still could not win congressional passage. However, several of its major proposals were enacted as five separate new laws, together known as the Compromise of 1850. These were signed into law by President Millard Fillmore in September 1850.

The main provisions of the five new laws were that:

The Nashville Convention

The laws of the Compromise of 1850 (see p. 42) were not viewed as compromises at all by either southern proslavery forces or northern antislavery forces. In the end, they were pushed through by a "swing" group of moderates from both North and South. This temporarily succeeded in stopping the breakup of the Union.

While the Compromise of 1850 was working its way through Congress, leading politicians from nine southern states held the Nashville Convention in Tennessee in June 1850. Opposing Henry Clay's Omnibus Bill, then before Congress, the delegates made their own proposals. These were far more favorable to the South than those presented by Clay.

After Congress adopted the main elements of Clay's compromise, the great majority of those who had met at Nashville very strongly objected to four of the five new laws making up the Compromise. For these proslavery Southerners only the new Fugitive Slave Act was acceptable. The other laws were unacceptable—and the Southerners' remedy was to call for destruction of the Union.

In November, six weeks after the five Compromise of 1850 bills had been signed into law, the Nashville Convention met again. It issued a call for the South to secede from the Union. Although many Southerners favored immediate secession, many other moderate Southerners sought to find a way to save the Union, while holding on to slavery.

Several southern state conventions refused to go along with the Nashville Convention's call to secede. Secession was blocked for another decade. Yet secession and the Civil War were coming closer.

- California would be admitted as a free state. California, which had already banned slavery in 1849, was admitted into the Union in 1850 (see Vol. 4, p. 68).
- New Mexico would have the choice of being admitted as a free or slave state. New Mexico would not be admitted into the Union until 1912, long after the issue had been settled by the Civil War.
- Utah would have the choice of being admitted as a free or slave state. Utah would be admitted into the Union in 1896.
- The slave trade would be abolished in the District of Columbia. This home of the nation's capital had since the early 1800s been a center of the domestic slave trade (see p. 12).

- The U.S. government would become deeply involved in catching escaped slaves under the Fugitive Slave Act.

The Fugitive Slave Act of 1850 provided that escaped slaves must be quickly returned to their owners without jury trials or the right to testify in their own defense. It also provided heavy penalties for Whites who helped them escape or gave them shelter. It further went on to provide that federal commissioners who ruled that slaves must be returned would receive $10 for each slave returned. However, they would only receive $5 for each slave captured but not returned.

The Fugitive Slave Act introduced a new era of widely detested slave catching and prosecutions. It was immediately denounced throughout the North. It also inspired Harriet Beecher Stowe to write the tremendously influential antislavery book *Uncle Tom's Cabin* (see p. 48).

Many northern states refused to enforce the law. This produced a number of highly inflammatory cases during the run-up to the Civil War, helping to develop even stronger antislavery feelings in the North.

Under the Fugitive Slave Act, this escaped slave was captured in the North and returned to slaveholders in the South.

Resisting the Fugitive Slave Act

African Americans such as Thomas Sims and Anthony Burns were captured by slave catchers in Boston, Massachusetts, with the aid of hundreds of federal officers. Their return to the South and slavery generated widespread protests in the 1850s.

In the North there was fierce and growing resistance to enforcement of the new federal Fugitive Slave Act. By the early 1850s antislavery sentiment in the North had grown tremendously. In case after case slave catchers found themselves sharply and often forcibly resisted by antislavery Northerners. The work of the Underground Railroad drew more and more Northerners (see p. 32), the numbers of escaping slaves grew, and many cases were nationally publicized, fueling resistance even more.

State governments also joined in resisting the Fugitive Slave Act. Some northern states adopted "personal liberty laws," aimed at stopping slave catchers and slave owners from kidnapping African Americans. Some of these laws were partly patterned on earlier protective state laws. For example, Indiana in 1824 and Connecticut in 1838 had passed laws requiring jury trials for those accused of being fugitive slaves.

The U.S. Supreme Court had opened the door wide to state personal liberty laws.

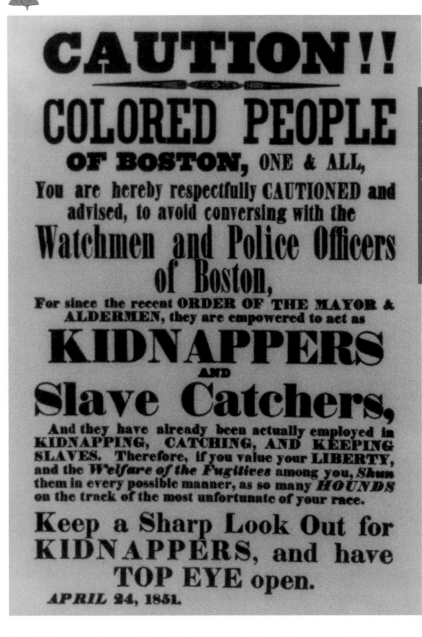

CAUTION!!
COLORED PEOPLE
OF BOSTON, ONE & ALL,
You are hereby respectfully CAUTIONED and advised, to avoid conversing with the
Watchmen and Police Officers of Boston,
For since the recent ORDER OF THE MAYOR & ALDERMEN, they are empowered to act as
KIDNAPPERS
AND
Slave Catchers,
And they have already been actually employed in KIDNAPPING, CATCHING, AND KEEPING SLAVES. Therefore, if you value your LIBERTY, and the *Welfare of the Fugitives* among you, *Shun* them in every possible manner, as so many *HOUNDS* on the track of the most unfortunate of your race.
Keep a Sharp Look Out for KIDNAPPERS, and have TOP EYE open.
APRIL 24, 1851.

This 1852 handbill warns African Americans in Boston to beware of slave catchers. Even African Americans born free would sometimes be taken by slave catchers because in many states they had no legal way to prove their freedom.

In *Prigg v. Pennsylvania* (1842), the Court ruled that the states were not required to help return fugitive slaves. This made their return very difficult, for then slave catchers and owners often found it impossible to overcome determined local resistance.

The Fugitive Slave Act of 1850 supplied federal commissioners and, if needed, federal law officers and troops to capture those accused of being escaped slaves. However, the states were still able to make that a very difficult task. In addition to the right to a jury trial, some state personal liberty laws also required full and convincing identification as well as proof of ownership. States could prosecute people who committed kidnappings and other illegal acts while claiming or taking African Americans. More than a dozen states adopted personal liberty laws before the Civil War, including Massachusetts, Connecticut, Michigan, and Wisconsin.

Even with the Underground Railroad and the personal liberty laws, slave catchers supported by federal forces were able to take many African Americans. One of the most notable cases was that of Thomas Sims, arrested in Boston in 1851. He was imprisoned and returned to Georgia, with the aid of hundreds of armed federal officers. However, thousands of people turned out in Boston to nonviolently protest the action. The resulting blaze of public anger traveled throughout the North. In 1854 the same situation again occurred in Boston, when escaped slave Anthony Burns was returned to Richmond, Virginia. This time, thousands of federal troops took him through the protesters, who were again nonviolent.

Nonviolence was only one means of protest as the long arguments over slavery and secession moved toward civil war. In 1851 thousands of antislavery protesters attacked a courthouse in Syracuse, New York. They freed imprisoned fugitive slave William Henry, who later made his way to Canada and freedom.

Estimates vary, but at least 10,000 slaves escaped to the North in the decade before the Civil War. Only an estimated 1,000 were returned to the South.

In the same period some thousands of slaves continued to escape to Mexico, although no good estimate is available of how many escaped. Many in the South, especially in Texas, tried to fight their way into Mexico in large groups. Others escaped to join Comanche and other Native-American peoples and later found their way to Mexico.

Escaped slaves were hunted by slave catchers with guns and dogs, as shown here.

Uncle Tom's Cabin

*This scene from **Uncle Tom's Cabin** shows Little Eva, daughter of a slave owner, converting to Christianity another little girl named Topsy, born a slave.*

Harriet Beecher Stowe's 1852 novel *Uncle Tom's Cabin* played a major role in the developing battle over slavery and secession. An abolitionist, Stowe wrote the book in response to the Fugitive Slave Act—and in the heat of the anger and revulsion felt throughout the North as slave catchers, with federal help, pursued African Americans accused of being fugitive slaves.

Stowe's novel told the story of a kindly, gentle slave named Tom, who eventually is whipped to death by sadistic slave owner Simon Legree—and of several other innocents, some of whom lived in terrible conditions under slavery. Some died, like "Uncle Tom"; others lived to escape to freedom.

The book was a highly emotional, extremely effective indictment of the whole system of slavery and of southern life. It was an extraordinary success in the North and ultimately throughout the world. It sold 300,000 copies in the first three months after its publication and 1 million copies in its first year. It went on to sell many millions of copies in many languages.

Southerners intensely disliked the novel, which they said was inaccurate and aimed at inflaming public opinion against slavery and against the South. And so it did. It cost the South any further hope of regaining the moral "high ground" on slavery. It also helped set northern public opinion very firmly against slavery at a time when the North and South were headed toward war.

In her novel Uncle Tom's Cabin, *Harriet Beecher Stowe captured the North's anger and revulsion over slavery and the hunting of fugitive slaves. Her work drew many people to the antislavery movement—so many that when President Abraham Lincoln first met her during the Civil War, he said: "Is this the little woman who made this great war?"*

The fame of Uncle Tom's Cabin *spread around the world. This plate painted with a scene from the novel, showing Uncle Tom being led away, was made in France.*

Southern plantation owners grew rich from slavery, building great houses like this one at Greenwood Plantation near New Orleans, Louisiana. But some managed—or tried—to convince themselves that slavery also benefited African Americans.

The Southern View of Slavery

In the early years of the United States, many Southerners had publicly and privately said that they looked forward to the end of slavery. Yet as the crisis over slavery and secession grew, southern support for slavery became much more intense. Earlier, such leaders as Washington and Jefferson—both of whom held slaves—had said they were against slavery, and had looked forward to ending slavery in the future. Now such voices were silent.

Earlier, many of slavery's defenders had called it an economic necessity for the South. However, they did not defend it on moral grounds, but instead weakly apologized for it.

All that changed quite rapidly when slavery came under sharp and sometimes successful attack. With the growth of slave revolts, the South became an armed camp. The lives of slaves became even more tightly controlled, and fear of massive revolts to come gripped the region.

As antislavery sentiment grew in the North, along with powerful, openly antislavery parties, Southerners' fear of being overwhelmed by the free states grew. As northern industrial power and population grew, so did southern fears that in a civil war the South would stand little chance of victory over the far more powerful North.

Proslavery southern political, religious, and educational leaders responded to those fears by dropping any apologies for slavery. Rewards were offered for the capture of such abolitionist leaders as William Lloyd Garrison and Arthur Tappan (see p. 29). Major American churches, including the Baptists and Methodists, split into northern and southern wings. Abolitionist writings were banned and sometimes burned in the South. Whites suspected of being anything but proslavery were physically attacked, often driven out of their communities, and in some cases killed.

Many Southerners came to see slavery as a fine and positive thing for slaveholders and—they said—for slaves. That view was supported by a wide range of speeches, books, and pamphlets, written by some of the most respectable people in the South. Now the right to own slaves was widely seen as an absolute moral right, far more important than preserving the Union.

Many went on to call for the international slave trade to be revived. In 1859 the Vicksburg Commercial Convention, held in Mississippi, called for restarting the international slave trade, banned since 1807.

The Election of 1852

As the presidential election of 1852 approached, the Whig Party found itself splitting into three groups, though it did not formally split apart. Some antislavery northern Whigs were "Conscience Whigs," who could not support the Compromise of 1850. Other northern Whigs, including President Millard Fillmore, continued to support the Compromise of 1850. They believed the Compromise to be the road to power and at the same time a way of saving the Union from secession. Proslavery southern Whigs, sometimes called "Cotton Whigs," supported slavery.

The net result of the split was that the Whigs were split in the North and very weak in the South. They passed over Fillmore and instead nominated General Winfield Scott of Mexican-American War fame for the Presidency. Scott ran a weak campaign, trying to please all groups by supporting the Compromise.

At the Democratic nominating convention of 1852, none of the three leading can-

This is a view of Washington, D.C., in 1852, shortly before the election of Franklin Pierce as President. In the foreground is the U.S. Capitol, high on a hill, with Pennsylvania Avenue leading off into the distance. The Potomac River and the Washington Monument, then still being built, are in the left background.

Franklin Pierce

Franklin Pierce (1804–1869) was the 14th President of the United States (1853–1857). A lawyer, soldier, and politician, he was the son of New Hampshire governor Benjamin Pierce.

Born in Hillsborough, New Hampshire, Pierce was a graduate of Bowdoin College. A Democrat, he served in the New Hampshire legislature (1829–1832), the House of Representatives (1833–1836), and the Senate (1837–1842). He was a brigadier general during the Mexican-American War. In 1852 he was nominated for the Presidency as a compromise candidate, after the three major candidates (Stephen Douglas, Lewis Cass, and James Buchanan) deadlocked in the Democratic nominating convention. Pierce was a largely ineffective President—so much so that his party declined to nominate him again in 1856. He then retired from public life.

Democratic candidate Franklin Pierce was elected President in 1852, after the Whig Party split apart. This is an 1853 portrait of him by George Peter Alexander Healy.

didates—Stephen Douglas, Lewis Cass, and James Buchanan—was able to win a majority. Franklin Pierce of New Hampshire won nomination as a "dark horse" candidate. The Free Soil Party nominated John P. Hale.

Pierce won the election with a landslide 254 electoral votes to Scott's 42 electoral votes. Hale won no electoral votes. The Free Soil Party passed from the national scene after this election and later merged with the new Republican Party (see p. 68).

In 1853, with China's experience in mind, Japan "opened" itself to the West. This is Matthew Calbraith Perry's expedition to Japan landing at Gorohama that year.

The Opening of Japan

Although slavery was by far the most dominant issue of the time, the United States continued to seek expansion during the Pierce Presidency.

In the Far East that expansion took the form of joining the European powers in their attack on a weakened China. That country had been "opened" by its defeat in the First Opium War (1840–1842) and the "unequal treaties" that followed (see Vol. 4,

p. 12). The United States would also go on to benefit from the unequal treaties that followed China's defeat in the Second Opium War (1860). China was in no condition to resist European and American attack, for it was being torn apart by the Taiping Rebellion (1850–1866), a massive Chinese civil war that cost 20 million to 40 million lives.

Japan still resisted Western penetration.

提督ペルリ省像

寅六十才

This is a Japanese woodblock portrait of Commodore Matthew Calbraith Perry, who led the American opening of Japan. He was the son of War of 1812 naval hero Oliver Hazard Perry.

It had been largely closed to the world since 1637, when all but a few foreigners were expelled from the country after a long civil war. However, the example of China made it clear that the Japanese armed forces would not be able to defend the country's coastal cities against the guns of Western warships.

On July 8, 1853, an American flotilla of four ships, commanded by Commodore Matthew Perry, sailed into Tokyo Bay. Unable to resist, the Japanese decided to "open" to the world. Japan and the United States began trade relations with the Treaty of Kanagawa (1854). Four years later Japan and the United States signed the Harris Treaty, an "unequal treaty" negotiated by U.S. consul Townsend Harris. Many other European nations soon followed the American lead, forcing unequal treaties on Japan.

The most notable proslavery filibuster leader was William Walker. He took power in Nicaragua in 1855 and ruled for two years before being defeated by a coalition of other Central American countries.

Filibusters South

Even after the Treaty of Guadalupe Hidalgo had been signed (see Vol. 4, p. 34), many Americans—most of them proslavery Southerners—wanted to annex all or most of what remained of Mexico. They did buy an additional piece of it in the Gadsden Purchase (see p. 57). Many also wanted to annex much of the Caribbean and Central America. They publicly declared, and some believed, that further expansion was part of the doctrine of manifest destiny (see Vol. 4, p. 14). That view was certainly shared by President Franklin Pierce, who repeatedly tried to buy Cuba from Spain.

Antislavery Northerners did not at all share that view. They saw such expansion as part of a southern drive to acquire territories that could be brought into the Union as slave states.

As the struggle over slavery and secession deepened, northern opposition to the doctrine of manifest destiny grew. The doctrine became increasingly unpopular and did not regain great popularity until the end of the century.

What did take place in the 1850s were several privately run attempts to expand southward. These attempts, called *filibusters,* all failed in the long run.

The most important of these was an

attempt to organize an invasion of Cuba, led by John Quitman, a former governor of Mississippi. President Pierce probably encouraged Quitman in the early stages of his planned invasion. However, faced with sharp northern opposition, Pierce changed his position and stopped Quitman's planned invasion before it could get started. The entire effort backfired, as Pierce then also ended his attempts to buy Cuba from Spain.

Another notable filibuster leader was American William Walker. In 1855 he led an expedition that seized power in Nicaragua. During his two years in power in that country, he reinstated slavery. Walker was defeated in 1857 by a Central American coalition that included Costa Rica, El Salvador, Honduras, and Guatemala. Captured while trying to return to Nicaragua in 1860, Walker was executed by the Honduran government.

The Gadsden Purchase

Much of the area of the Gadsden Purchase was desert country, like this scene dominated by a large saguaro cactus.

American government pressure on Mexico to cede more territory continued after the Treaty of Guadalupe Hidalgo ended the Mexican-American War (see Vol. 4, p. 34). U.S. railroad company pressure to get Mexican land for a southern railway route was strong, and the South was anxious to establish a southern transcontinental route.

With little ability to resist, the Mexican government soon gave way. On December 30, 1853, in the Gadsden Treaty ("Gadsden Purchase"), the United States acquired almost 30,000 square miles of northern Mexico, in what became southern Arizona and New Mexico (see map in Vol. 2, p. 60). The U.S. government agreed to pay Mexico $15 million for the territory. It later cut the payment to $10 million, and defeated Mexico agreed to the cut.

Political storms raged over whether Kansas and other western states and territories would be slave or free. Meanwhile individual families, like this one in Kansas, faced life-and-death issues such as drought and possible starvation.

The Kansas-Nebraska Act

The coming storm came much closer on May 30, 1854. That was the day that President Franklin Pierce signed the Kansas-Nebraska Act, which repealed the Missouri Compromise of 1820 (see Vol. 3, p. 58). The new law set in motion a series of increasingly violent clashes between pro-slavery and antislavery forces. It also caused a major reorganization of American political parties, leading directly to secession and war.

Illinois Democratic Senator Stephen Douglas sponsored the Kansas-Nebraska Act and pushed it through Congress. He had not intended to create a crisis. Far from it. A strong expansionist, he sought a compromise that would get northern and southern votes for a transcontinental railroad route through the huge Nebraska Territory.

Douglas proposed to split the Nebraska Territory into the new Kansas and Nebraska territories. He planned to put the railroad through what would become the new slave state of Kansas, with Nebraska becoming a free state.

Douglas's plan would effectively repeal the Missouri Compromise, because under the terms of that Compromise, the whole of Kansas and Nebraska would be free, not slave. Instead, Douglas proposed to let each new state decide for itself whether it would be slave or free, as provided in the Utah and New Mexico portions of the Compromise of 1850 (see p. 42). He called this "popular sovereignty"; some others called it "squatter sovereignty." This same doctrine had been put forward by Democratic presidential candidate Lewis Cass in 1848; it had then been called "state sovereignty" (see p. 39).

As quickly became apparent, the Douglas bill set off a huge North-South argument, for the Missouri Compromise was central to the balance of the nation. In return for its support, the South insisted that Douglas publicly state that his bill would repeal and replace the Missouri Compromise. He did so, with the support of President Pierce.

The antislavery North responded with enormous anger. However, the Democrats remained mainly united for the time being, with many northern Democrats joining southern Democrats to vote for the bill. The Whigs, on the other hand, suffered a sharp North-South split, especially in the House of Representatives. The shape of a different future began to appear in American politics.

The Missouri Compromise had been repealed and replaced by "popular sovereignty," which solved nothing. Instead of a stable compromise between proslavery and antislavery forces, the nation was plunged into a bloody war in Kansas over whether Kansas would enter the Union as a free or a slave state (see p. 70). That conflict joined the growing North-South battles over the Fugitive Slave Act. It would soon be joined by other major events on the now-short road to secession and war.

Stephen Douglas, Democratic Senator from Illinois, crafted the Kansas-Nebraska Act and engineered its passage in Congress. The result was to widen the split between North and South.

In the years before the Civil War, the Pony Express was one of the few ways to communicate quickly—that is, within a couple of weeks or less—between the East and distant California. Here a rider is arriving to find a fresh horse awaiting him.

The Transcontinental Routes

During the years of crisis that followed the Kansas-Nebraska Act, Senator Stephen Douglas's plan to build a transcontinental railroad could not be accomplished. That would have to wait until after the Civil War. The first transcontinental railroad would be completed on May 10, 1869, when the Union Pacific and Central Pacific railways were joined with the driving of a "golden spike" at Promontory Point, Utah.

Yet in the years before the Civil War, some sort of transcontinental communications route remained a major United States goal. At stake was California, which was hotly contested by proslavery and antislavery forces, even though its new population leaned more against slavery. The North was determined to establish a north-central transcontinental route that would pass through free territory in the event of war. The South was just as determined to block a northern route and to establish a southern route to California.

During the final run-up to the Civil War, two major attempts were made to establish transcontinental communications routes: the Butterfield Stage line and the Pony Express.

The Butterfield Stage

The Butterfield Stage (Butterfield Southern Overland Mail Route) was authorized by Congress in 1857. It started operations in September 1858 after an intense North-South fight in Congress. In the end, the South won the argument, for Postmaster General Aaron V. Brown, a Southerner, had legal control of the choice. He picked a southern route that led from St. Louis, Missouri, and Memphis, Tennessee, through El Paso, Texas, and Tucson, Arizona, to San Francisco, California. The South's victory lasted only until the Civil

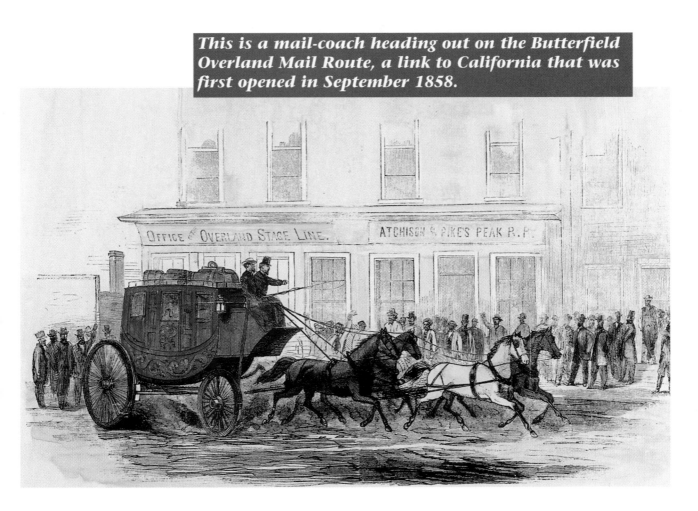

This is a mail-coach heading out on the Butterfield Overland Mail Route, a link to California that was first opened in September 1858.

PONY EXPRESS!

CHANGE OF TIME!   REDUCED RATES!

10 Days to San Francisco!

LETTERS

WILL BE RECEIVED AT THE

OFFICE, 84 BROADWAY,

NEW YORK,

Up to 4 P. M. every TUESDAY.

AND

Up to 2½ P. M. every SATURDAY,

Which will be forwarded to connect with the PONY EXPRESS leaving ST. JOSEPH, Missouri,

Every WEDNESDAY and SATURDAY at 11 P. M.

TELEGRAMS

Sent to Fort Kearney on the mornings of MONDAY and FRIDAY, will connect with PONY leaving St. Joseph, WEDNESDAYS and SATURDAYS.

EXPRESS CHARGES.

LETTERS weighing half ounce or under $1.00
For every additional half ounce or fraction of an ounce 1.00
In all cases to be enclosed in 10 cent Government Stamped Envelopes,
And all Express CHARGES Pre-paid.

☞ PONY EXPRESS ENVELOPES For Sale at our Office.

WELLS, FARGO & CO., Ag'ts.

New York, July 1, 1861.

This poster—dated July 1, 1861—promises delivery of letters from New York to California in 10 days. In reality, it could sometimes take longer, though sometimes as little as eight days.

The Pony Express

The second transcontinental communications route opened up by the United States before the Civil War was the Pony Express, one of the best-known and most exciting features of the American West.

The Pony Express was the first fast transcontinental mail service. Starting at St. Joseph, Missouri, it generally followed the route of the Oregon and California Trails from there to Fort Bridger. It then took a more southerly route that went south

War. Then the route was changed to keep it entirely in Union territory.

The stage service traveled west twice each week and took 25 days from St. Louis to San Francisco. After the transcontinental railroad was completed in 1869, the transcontinental portion of the stage line would go out of service. However, many of the stage lines connected to it after the Civil War remained in service for decades.

to Salt Lake City, Utah, there joining the California Trail to Sacramento, California (see map in Vol. 4, p. 48).

The Pony Express trip from St. Joseph to Sacramento took varying amounts of time, depending on such matters as weather and Native-American attacks on the way. The fastest time recorded was in November 1860, when Pony Express riders carried the news of Abraham Lincoln's election (see p. 83) from St. Joseph to Sacramento in a little less than eight days.

Pony Express service began on April 4, 1860. It lasted only 18 months, for it was soon overtaken by the transcontinental telegraph system. On October 24, 1861, the first transcontinental telegraph message, sent from Sacramento, California, to Washington, D.C., was received by President Abraham Lincoln in the White House. Very fast communication with the West had been achieved, and the Pony Express was discontinued.

At stage stops along the route, Pony Express riders would quickly change horses and speed on their way, as in this scene by Frederic Remington.

The Reshaping of American Politics

As the North-South split over slavery widened and deepened, the American political system began to reshape itself to reflect that split.

The first major casualty was the Whig Party. It had already split into three groups over the Compromise of 1850 (see p. 42). However, the Whigs could not recover from their second major split, over the Kansas-Nebraska Act (see p. 58). The Whigs soon began to dissolve. Those against slavery moved into new political parties. Those who remained, led by Millard Fillmore, had little strength left.

The Democrats, on the other hand, largely stayed together as a single—though far from united—party. It would split later on North-South lines.

Meanwhile in the mid-1850s two new parties emerged: the Know-Nothing (American) Party (see p. 65) and the Republican Party (see p. 68).

This is a copy of a delegate's electoral card for the American Party, organized by Know-Nothings in 1853. Its slogan was "America for Americans."

The Know-Nothings

Like the Anti-Masonic Party of the 1840s, the Know-Nothing Party was to a large extent part of the history of bigotry in American society (see Vol. 3, p. 75). At the same time it was—for a short time in the mid-1850s—a powerful new political party. In one period it even seemed about to be voted into national power.

The Know-Nothing Party, the name by which it was best known, began its life in 1849, as a small secret society named the Order of the Star-Spangled Banner. In 1853 the Know-Nothings organized a new political party, officially named the American Party. The party was also sometimes known as the Native American Party, for its members were "nativists," best described as demanding an "America for Americans."

Like the earlier Anti-Masonic Party, the Know-Nothings saw conspiracies everywhere. Their favorite targets were the Catholic Church and Irish Catholic Americans. They also made targets of several other kinds of immigrants, including the German immigrants who were then beginning to arrive in substantial numbers.

In the years since then, describing someone as a "Know-Nothing" has become a way of accusing others of ignorance and bigotry. However, the party came to be called "Know-Nothing" because its members, when asked anything about it, responded "I know nothing," or "I know nothing about it."

The Know-Nothings—sometimes called nativists—took Native Americans as a symbol, as shown in this advertisement for "Know Nothing Soap." Their main targets were people who were foreign-born, such as the Irish (especially Catholic Irish) and German immigrants who were then arriving in large numbers.

This young fellow was known as "Uncle Sam's youngest son Citizen Know Nothing." His dashing, attractive image was designed to attract supporters for the Know-Nothings' stand against new immigrants.

Many antislavery former Whigs (some of whom had earlier been Anti-Masonic Party members) found a new political home in the Know-Nothing Party. So did many proslavery southern Whigs, who were leaving their now very weak party—even though in the early 1850s the Know-Nothings described themselves as antislavery.

Yet the Know-Nothing appeal went far beyond former Whigs. Their nativism attracted large numbers of voters, most of them United States–born Protestants, especially in New England and the West. At the same time their antislavery stance attracted many throughout the North, who wanted to vote for a strong new antislavery party.

After passage of the Kansas-Nebraska Act, the Know-Nothings had a tremendous surge of sup-port and quickly organized themselves into a powerful national party. In the state elections of 1854 they elected a Know-Nothing governor of Massachusetts and a majority in the Massachusetts state legislature. They also made strong showings in New York and several other states. Their prospects seemed very bright indeed.

Yet the issue of slavery destroyed those prospects. In 1855 the southern wing of the party pushed through resolutions favoring slavery at the Know-Nothing national convention. Large numbers of antislavery Know-Nothings immediately left the party. Know-Nothing support swiftly sank throughout the country. In the presidential campaign of 1856, their candidate was former president Millard Fillmore, who carried only the state of Maryland.

> *I am not a Know-Nothing. . . . How could I be? How can anyone who abhors the oppression of Negroes be in favor of degrading classes of white people? . . . When the Know-Nothings get control, it [the Constitution] will read "all men are created equal, except Negroes and foreigners and Catholics."*
>
> ABRAHAM LINCOLN, IN A LETTER,
> AUGUST 24, 1855

The first presidential candidate nominated by the Republican Party would be John C. Frémont, famed for his expeditions in the West, in 1856.

The Republican Party

In the national crisis that followed passage of the Kansas-Nebraska Act (see p. 58), a new alternative soon emerged for those who opposed slavery. This was the antislavery Republican Party, soon to become the party of Abraham Lincoln.

After President Franklin Pierce signed the Kansas-Nebraska Act, new antislavery groups began to form throughout the North and West. Most of those forming the new organizations were former Whigs.

However, an estimated one third were former northern Democrats who were as unwilling as the Whigs to accept any extension of slavery into the territories. Also joining them were substantial numbers of angry, newly active antislavery Northerners and Westerners.

On July 9, 1854—only two months after the Kansas-Nebraska Act became law—a state antislavery convention in Michigan adopted the name "Republican." Four days

BUFFALO EXPRESS EXTRA.

NO MORE SLAVE TERRITORY

FREEDOM, FREE SPEECH, FREE KANSAS & FREMONT!
Against BUCHANAN, FILLMORE, DOUGHFACEISM, SLAVERY, and the BORDER RUFFIANS!

The Republican party is organized upon the platform of LIBERTY, Independence and equal rights, as embodied in the Declaration of Independence and the Constitution of the United States, to maintain the union of the States and the rights of the States; Freedom of Speech and of the Press—to resist the spread of slavery and the aggressions of the slave power. The equal rights of all persons to impartial protection in the enjoyment of religious freedom, and of all American Citizens, whether native or naturalized, to the free exercise of the elective franchise, and the enjoyment of its benefits; and we propose no tests for office, except honesty, capacity and devotion to American institutions.

We maintain that there shall be no slavery outside the slave states, and no domination over the National Government by the slave power; and for this purpose have nominated

For President, JOHN C. FREMONT.
Vice " WM. L. DAYTON.

PLATFORM OF FREEDOM!
Adopted by the REPUBLICAN CONVENTION at Philadelphia, June 18th, 1856.

"This Convention of Delegates, assembled in pursuance of a call addressed to the people of the United States without regard to past political differences or divisions, who are opposed to the repeal of the Missouri Compromise; to the policy of the present Administration; to the extension of slavery into free Territory, in favor of the admission of Kansas as a Free State; of restoring the action of the Federal Government to the principles of Washington and Jefferson; and for the purpose of presenting candidates for the offices of President and Vice President, do

"1. *Resolve*, That the maintenance of the principles promulgated in the Declaration of Independence and embodied in the Federal Constitution are essential to the preservation of our Republican institutions, and that the Federal Constitution, the rights of the States, and the union of the States shall be preserved.

"2. *Resolved*, That with our Republican fathers we hold it to be a self evident truth that all men are endowed with the unalienable right to life, liberty and the pursuit of happiness, and that the primary object and ulterior design of our Federal Government were to secure those rights to all persons within its exclusive jurisdiction; that as our Republican fathers, when they had abolished Slavery in all our National Territory, ordained that no person should be deprived of life, liberty, or property, without due process of law, it be-

The new Republican Party, with John C. Frémont as their first nominee for the Presidency, staked out its political position in opposition to slavery. It was supported by antislavery newspapers around the country, such as this 1856 editorial, "No More Slave Territory," from the Buffalo Express.

won 108 of the 234 seats in the House of Representatives, with the Democrats holding on to only 83 seats in the House. In the Senate the Republicans won 15 of the 60 seats, with the Democrats holding on to 40. The Republicans then immediately began to look forward to the 1856 presidential election.

The Republican Party viewed itself as the logical successor to Thomas Jefferson's earlier Democratic-Republican Party (see Vol. 2, p. 20). They accordingly named themselves Republicans. They credited Jefferson with winning the fight to ban slavery in the territories created by the Northwest Ordinance of 1787, beginning the political side of the antislavery cause, and modeled themselves on his example. Andrew Jackson had renamed the earlier Republican Party, calling it the Democratic Party; now there was another Republican Party in the United States.

later, on July 13, several more state conventions did the same, accepting that name for their new party.

The new political party quickly became a national party, though all of its strength was in the North and West. The Republicans ran candidates throughout the North and West in the autumn 1854 congressional elections. They came out of those elections as a major force on the national scene: They

Missourians known as "Border Ruffians" invaded Kansas in the 1850s on the pro-slavery side, when the territory was to choose between slave and free.

Bleeding Kansas

Small-scale civil war came to Kansas in 1854, seven years before the storm broke in the rest of the country. The conflict began in the spring of 1854, after passage of the Kansas-Nebraska Act (see p. 58), over whether to bring the new Territory into the Union as a slave state or a free one.

The great majority of the people who had settled in Kansas and who were still arriving there were antislavery Northerners, from many parts of the North and West. Added to these were an estimated 2,000 more antislavery settlers, organized by the New England Anti-Slavery Society (see p. 30).

Most of the proslavery forces were from bordering Missouri. Many of these were popularly known as "Border Ruffians," a term that came to be used for all of the proslavery people in Kansas.

Being so much closer to Kansas, most of the Missourians arrived there sooner than the New Englanders. Far more important to the way the struggle developed was the fact that the proslavery forces proved ready to use any means to achieve power.

This is Lawrence, Kansas, after it was attacked by proslavery forces, as part of the statewide civil war over whether Kansas would become a slave state or a free one.

In May 1855 proslavery forces "won" the first Kansas territorial election, which was accompanied by massive fraud and violence. An estimated 5,000 Missourians had invaded Kansas, and most of them had voted in the election even though ineligible to do so. The winners then organized a proslavery territorial government at Lecompton, Kansas, and passed proslavery laws meant to destroy all opposition.

In response, the antislavery majority organized the Free State army at Big Springs, Kansas, in September 1855. In October they set up a competing territorial government in Topeka, Kansas. A leader of the Free State forces was John Brown, who had been an agent of the Underground Railroad (see p. 32).

Lawrence, Kansas, became one of the centers of the conflict over the Territory. In late November 1855 an estimated 1,500 armed Missourians moved to attack Lawrence. They broke off when they found the city defended by Free State forces. On May 21, 1856, the Missourians did attack and sack Lawrence, which was then very lightly defended. Four days after the sack of Lawrence, on May 25, 1856, John Brown led an attack that killed five proslavery settlers on Pottawatomie Creek, Kansas.

The Missourians' attack on Lawrence and Brown's killings at Pottawatomie inflamed already strong sentiments on both sides—in Kansas and throughout the country. More than a year of undeclared civil war followed in Kansas, resulting in an estimated 200 dead and a much larger number of casualties. Congress refused to accept either of the two competing Kansas governments, and the Territory had no effective government during that period.

In October 1857 Kansas elected a Free State legislature. On October 19 the Lecompton Constitutional Convention adopted a new, proslavery state constitution. That constitution was approved in a fraudulent statewide popular vote. It was then rejected by a wide margin in a second statewide popular vote, this one organized by the Free State Party.

The Lecompton Constitution then went to the U.S. Congress, which was deadlocked on its acceptance. The Constitution was sent back to Kansas for a third statewide popular vote. In early 1858 the Lecompton Constitution was decisively rejected by Kansas voters, who went on to vote in an antislavery constitution in the fall of 1859. However, southern opposition in the U.S. Congress then blocked the admission of Kansas into the Union until 1861.

This is an image from a so-called "Peace Convention" held at Fort Scott, Kansas, as part of the Free Soil slave-or-free debate of the 1850s.

In 1858, the date of this image, the grounds of the White House were still open to the public, and people could walk there freely.

The Buchanan Presidency

As the presidential election of 1856 approached, the Democratic Party and its supporters managed to hold together—although its northern and southern wings were increasingly far apart on the questions of slavery and secession. As antislavery forces in the North continued to gain strength and hold the moral high ground, many southern states were clearly preparing to secede. Some Democrats in the North were going over to the new Repub-

lican Party, but most were still prepared to try to stay in the Democratic Party and to try to preserve the Union.

The Democrats nominated former secretary of state James Buchanan of Pennsylvania for the Presidency. He ran as a moderate who would take no position on slavery, the great issue facing the country.

The new Republican Party, in its first presidential election, ran western explorer John C. Frémont of California. Former president Millard Fillmore was the candidate of what remained of the Whig and Know-Nothing parties.

James Buchanan was elected as the 15th President of the United States (1857–1861), with 174 electoral votes to 114 for Frémont and only 8 for Fillmore.

The Buchanan Presidency was entirely dominated by the joined issues of slavery and secession. The Supreme Court's Dred Scott decision (see p. 75), the continuing undeclared civil war in Kansas (see p. 70), and John Brown's raid on Harpers Ferry (see p. 80) all focused national attention on those issues.

Antislavery Northerners saw Buchanan as a proslavery President, at all times willing to do the bidding of southern slaveholders. At the same time, Southerners—increasingly ready to secede—suspected Buchanan, for he spoke against secession and for preserving the Union. In any event, he showed no ability to lead the nation as the final crisis of slavery and secession approached.

James Buchanan

President James Buchanan showed little ability to lead the country at a time when strong leadership was vitally necessary.

James Buchanan (1791–1868) was the 15th President of the United States (1857–1861). A lawyer, politician, and diplomat, he was the last American President before the Civil War.

Born in Mercersburg, Pennsylavania, Buchanan practiced law (1812–1814) before beginning his political career in the Pennsylvania state legislature (1814–1816). A Democrat, he served in the House of Representatives (1820–1831), was Minister to Russia (1832–1833), and then served in the Senate (1834–1845). He was Secretary of State (1845–1851) and Minister to Britain (1853–1856) before becoming President. An opponent of secession, he supported the Union during the Civil War.

Dred Scott sued for his freedom after his owner had taken him to live in free states. The U.S. Supreme Court ruling against him would help trigger the Civil War.

The Dred Scott Decision

One of the final steps on the road to civil war was the U.S. Supreme Court decision in the case of *Dred Scott v. Sandford* (1857). Dred Scott was an African-American slave in Missouri during the 1830s. He had later been taken by his owner into the free state of Illinois and the free Wisconsin Territory, and later back to Missouri. Scott sued for his freedom in a federal court on the grounds that he had been set free because he had lived in territories of the United States from which slavery had been banned by the Missouri Compromise of 1820.

The Supreme Court, in its majority decision written by Chief Justice Roger Taney (see Vol. 3, p. 74), refused to set Scott free. Taney ruled that the Missouri Compromise was void because Congress did not have the constitutional power to enact it. He further ruled that the laws of Missouri applied, not those of Illinois, because Scott had later returned to

75

Missouri. Taney went on to rule that no African American, even though free, could become a citizen of the United States.

Taney, the rest of the Court's majority, and President James Buchanan had hoped to solve the massive argument over slavery that was splitting the country apart. They accomplished just the opposite.

The North was absolutely unwilling to accept destruction of the Missouri Compromise and to reopen the question of slavery in many territories that had already been guaranteed entry into the Union as free states. Nor was the North willing to raise the question of slavery once again in states and territories already in the Union and free. Beyond that, the North was unwilling to forever deny citizenship to free African Americans.

The Dred Scott decision brought a storm of angry criticism from throughout the North, driving the North and South farther apart than ever before. In turn, the South's position hardened still more, as it became even clearer that slavery would be doomed as the free states of North grew in number, population, and power. The Republican Party developed new strength from the angry North. Meanwhile, the Democratic Party began to pull apart, as its southern wing prepared to secede and its northern wing moved to preserve the Union.

With the Dred Scott decision, Chief Justice of the U.S. Supreme Court Roger Taney helped split North and South even more over the questions of slavery and secession.

The debates between Abraham Lincoln and Stephen Douglas sharpened the differences between their positions and made Lincoln a national figure. Here Lincoln (standing) is speaking; Douglas is seated just to the left of him.

The Lincoln-Douglas Debates

"A house divided against itself cannot stand." I believe this government cannot endure permanently half slave and half free. I do not expect the Union to be dissolved—I do not expect the house to fall—but I do expect it will cease to be divided. It will become all one thing or all the other.

The above quotation is from the opening of Abraham Lincoln's first speech of his 1858 campaign for the U.S. Senate. It was delivered to the Illinois Republican state convention at Springfield, Illinois, on June 16, 1858.

As it turned out, it was far more than a single campaign speech by a relatively unknown western politician, for—from the start—Lincoln spoke to the whole nation. This was Abraham Lincoln emerging, the "Father Abraham" who would lead and preserve the Union through four terrible years of civil war, who would free the slaves and lose his life to an assassin at war's end. This was Abraham Lincoln emerging, who would stand with George Washington as the greatest of American

In the days before television and radio, people gathered by the hundreds to hear political debates, such as this one between Abraham Lincoln and Stephen Douglas at Galesburg, Illinois, in 1858.

Because Lincoln caught the attention of the nation from the first, and because Douglas was already a national figure, the election attracted great interest throughout the country. That interest became enormous during a series of seven debates—the famous Lincoln-Douglas debates—between the two candidates during the summer and fall of 1858.

The debates attracted large audiences in Illinois and a great deal of newspaper cov-

presidents and become a world figure and a symbol of all the best in America.

Lincoln's opponent—who won the election—was two-term Illinois Democratic Senator Stephen Douglas, the architect of the Kansas-Nebraska Act. He was the chief spokesperson for those Democrats and others, both North and South, who sought to preserve the Union while somehow satisfying both proslavery and antislavery forces. By 1858 that was highly unlikely but still very appealing to large numbers of Illinois voters.

> *As I would not be a slave, so I would not be a master. This expresses my idea of democracy. Whatever differs from this, to the extent of the difference, is no democracy.*
>
> ABRAHAM LINCOLN, AUGUST 1, 1858

erage throughout the country. They sharply defined the differences between two major points of view as to the future of the Union and brought Abraham Lincoln national prominence and the leadership of the Republican Party.

In the course of the debates, Douglas defended the "popular sovereignty" ideas put forward in his Kansas-Nebraska Act, allowing each new territory to choose on its own whether to be slave or free. At the same time he supported the Supreme Court's Dred Scott decision, which destroyed the Missouri Compromise of 1820. His basic view was that it was necessary to accept slavery anywhere in the country, rather than abolishing it, if the Union was to have any hope of being preserved.

Lincoln, on the other hand, attacked the Kansas-Nebraska Act and the Dred Scott decision. He held the view that the only way the Union could be preserved was by ending slavery and that slavery was above all wrong and impossible to justify or accept.

In his debates with Douglas, Lincoln took and held the high moral ground, just as antislavery forces were successfully doing on the issue of slavery throughout the North. Lincoln held that slavery and the principles of American democracy simply did not mix, and that they could not in any circumstances be made to mix. It was a simple, powerful argument. Though this argument did not win him the Illinois Senate seat in 1858, two years later it won Lincoln and the Republican Party the Presidency.

In the congressional elections of 1858, the still-new Republican Party won a majority in the House of Representatives, with a 113–101 victory over the Democrats. However, the Democrats held their majority in the Senate, with a 38–26 win over the Republicans.

Literally born in a log cabin, Lincoln was attractive to many Americans because of his home-spun style and humble beginnings. Here he is portrayed in an activity familiar to all frontier people: splitting logs for fence rails.

On October 17, 1859, the day after he began his attack on the federal arsenal at Harpers Ferry, Virginia, John Brown was captured.

Harpers Ferry

On October 16, 1859, a force of 22 armed men, led by John Brown, took the U.S. arsenal at Harpers Ferry, Virginia (now West Virginia), with its large stores of arms and ammunition. Fighting beside Brown were five African Americans and 16 Whites.

Brown's aim was to begin a massive slave revolt that would sweep the South and with it sweep away slavery. He planned to use the captured arsenal to equip what he believed would become a massive revolutionary army.

In this he was entirely wrong. Not one African American joined his small force after it had seized the arsenal. Instead, Virginia and Maryland militia units responded quickly, surrounding and besieging Brown's force, which was trapped in a railroad building on the arsenal's grounds.

The next day a force of U.S. Marines arrived, led by then-Colonel Robert E. Lee, who would later command Confederate forces during the Civil War. It included then-Lieutenant J. E. B. (Jeb) Stuart, a Confederate cavalry general during the Civil War. The marines stormed Brown's refuge, taking him and what remained of his force.

John Brown was a leading abolitionist in the years just before the Civil War and a commander of antislavery Free State forces in "Bleeding Kansas" in the late 1850s. In 1859 he led a raid on the federal arsenal at Harpers Ferry, Virginia, aiming to generate a widespread slave revolt in the South. Though it failed, his raid was a major event on the road to war.

In the first place, I deny everything but what I have all along admitted: of a design on my part to free slaves. . . .

Had I so interfered in behalf of the rich, the powerful, the intelligent, the so-called great, or in behalf of any of their friends . . . every man in this court would have deemed it an act worthy of reward rather than punishment.

I see a book kissed which I suppose to be the Bible, or at least the New Testament, which teaches me that all things whatsoever I would that men should do unto me, I should do even so to them. . . . I believe that to have interfered as I have done . . . in behalf of His despised poor, I did no wrong, but right. Now if it is deemed necessary that I should forfeit my life for the furtherance of the ends of justice and mingle my blood further with the blood of my children and with the blood of millions in this slave country whose rights are disregarded by wicked, cruel and unjust enactments, I say, let it be done.

JOHN BROWN, IN HIS LAST SPEECH TO THE COURT, NOVEMBER 2, 1859

Only one member of Brown's force escaped. All of the others, including Brown, died in battle or were afterward hanged. John Brown was hanged on December 2, 1859, at Charlestown, Virginia.

John Brown's attack on Harpers Ferry was the last great milestone on the road to secession and civil war. To the South he was nothing but a lawless murderer, who carried with him the seeds of the massive slave revolt Southerners had feared for generations.

A young African-American mother presented her child to John Brown, en route to his hanging.

Although Brown had, in fact, acted alone, the overwhelming majority of southern opinion was that he had been only the visible edge of a huge northern abolitionist conspiracy, led by the Republican Party. After John Brown's raid on Harpers Ferry, the South prepared for its own long-feared secession.

Reaction in the North was just the opposite. Although many publicly criticized Brown, antislavery Northerners saw him as a great martyr, who had been hanged for what was widely described as doing God's work. His cause now became the cause of many White Northerners, who had until then felt no personal stake in the fight against slavery.

In a little while the North would go to war, singing:

John Brown's body lies a-mouldering
   in the grave . . .
But his soul is marching on.
Glory, glory, hallelujah! His soul is
   marching on!

In 1862, during the Civil War, Julia Ward Howe would fit new words to the melody and name it "The Battle Hymn of the Republic," a song still turned to by Americans in times of crisis and war.

Abraham Lincoln was inaugurated on the steps of the U.S. Capitol on March 4, 1861. Seven states in the South had already seceded from the Union. The Civil War would begin just a month later.

The Election of 1860

As the 1860 presidential election approached, the Democratic Party split into northern and southern wings. Meanwhile, the South moved toward secession, and the united, antislavery Republican Party moved toward power.

For the Republicans, Abraham Lincoln once more spoke to a national audience. He set the tone for the presidential campaign and the war that would follow in his speech at Cooper Union in New York City on February 27, 1860. Lincoln made it clear that the Republican Party did not at that time call for abolishing slavery where it already existed, but that he and his party would not accept the further expansion of slavery simply because "slavery is wrong," which he said again and again. Lincoln then went on to issue a clear warning to the South, saying:

. . . let us stand by our duty, fearlessly and effectively . . . Neither let us be slandered from our duty by false accusations against us, nor frightened from it by menaces of destruction to the Government nor of dungeons to ourselves. Let us have faith that right makes might, and in that faith let us, to the end, dare to do our duty as we understand it.

83

Abraham Lincoln

Abraham Lincoln was a child of the American frontier, who symbolized all that was best in the American nation. In his generation and for generations then unborn, he was the President who saved the Union, the President who freed the slaves.

Lincoln (1809–1865) was the 16th President of the United States (1861–1865). He was born near Hodgenville, Kentucky, and grew up in Indiana and Illinois with very little money and hardly any formal education. In 1831 he settled at New Salem, near the Illinois state capital at Springfield, where he studied law part-time. He began to practice law in 1835.

Lincoln was a militia captain during the Black Hawk War (1834). He also began his political career that same year, serving in the Illinois state legislature (1834–1841), then going back to his law practice. He served in the U.S. Congress as a Whig for a single term (1847–1849) and again returned to the law, while staying active in politics. In 1855, still a

Abraham Lincoln was the first U.S. President to be elected from the new Republican Party, a party founded primarily by those opposed to slavery. This portrait was painted by John Henry Brown in 1860, the year of his election to the Presidency.

Whig, he made an unsuccessful run for the U.S. Senate.

In 1858 Lincoln ran for the Senate again, this time as a Republican. Although he lost the election to Stephen Douglas, Lincoln came out of the campaign a national figure (see p. 77). He went on to win the Presidency in 1860.

During the Civil War, Lincoln became the "Father Abraham" who won the fight to preserve the Union. He also became a world figure, whose Emancipation Proclamation (1863) ended slavery in the United States.

Lincoln was shot by John Wilkes Booth at Washington's Ford Theatre on April 14, 1865, and died the next morning.

The Lincoln Memorial, built in the early 20th century at one end of the Mall in Washington, D.C., has become a modern place of pilgrimage for many who honored the man and his beliefs. The Classical-style building has 36 columns, one for each state in the Union when Lincoln was President.

At the Republican National Convention in Chicago (May 16–18, 1860), Abraham Lincoln of Illinois was nominated for the Presidency on the third ballot, after supporters of abolitionist leaders William Seward and Salmon P. Chase deadlocked.

The Democrats Split

At the Democratic National Convention in Charleston, South Carolina (April 23, 1860), the delegates from the eight states of the Deep South walked out after the majority refused to adopt a platform that guaranteed slavery in the territories. Unable to agree on a presidential candidate, the convention then adjourned until it met again at Baltimore, Maryland, on June 18. There the convention nominated Stephen Douglas of Illinois for the Presidency.

However, the southern delegates left the Convention. Meeting again on June 28, in Baltimore, they nominated John C. Breckenridge of Kentucky for the Presidency.

A fourth presidential candidate was named by what remained of the Know-Nothings and Whigs. At Baltimore on May 9 they renamed themselves the Constitutional Union Party and nominated John Bell of Tennessee for the Presidency.

With four parties in the field and the Democrats split, the election of Lincoln was certain. On November 6 Abraham Lincoln was elected the 16th President of the United States, with a landslide 180 electoral votes, to 72 for Breckenridge, 39 for Bell, and 12 for Douglas. Lincoln's Vice President was Hannibal Hamlin of Maine.

Abraham Lincoln had come to Illinois as part of the major westward push of the early 19th century. Born in Kentucky in 1809, he moved with his family to Indiana in 1816 and then to Illinois in 1830. There they settled in this cabin, built by his father, Thomas Lincoln.

Secession and War

With Lincoln's election the secession of all or much of the South became certain. On December 20, 1860, more than two months before Lincoln's inauguration, South Carolina seceded from the Union. Two days later South Carolina began to seize federal government forts and arsenals in South Carolina, without resistance from federal troops. Five other states also quickly seceded from the Union: Mississippi (January 9, 1861), Florida (January 10), Alabama (January 11), Georgia (January 19), and Louisiana (January 26).

On February 4, 1861, the states that had seceded formed the Confederate States of America, with Jefferson Davis as President. On February 23 Texas seceded from the Union. Later in 1861 they would be joined by four other states: Arkansas (May 6), North Carolina (May 20), Virginia (May 23), and Tennessee (June 8).

Abraham Lincoln was inaugurated President on March 4, 1861. On April 4, 1861, at 4:30 A.M., Confederate shore batteries at Charleston, South Carolina, fired on Fort Sumter in Charleston's harbor, beginning the Civil War.

On the Internet

The Internet has many interesting and useful sites. However, the site addresses often change. The best way to find current addresses is to go to a search site, such as **www.yahoo.com**. As this book was being written, websites relating to this volume included:

http://memory.loc.gov/ammem/ndlpedu/features/timeline/expref/expand.html
National Expansion and Reform, 1815–1880, a section of the Library of Congress's American Memory site, offering activities and resources, plus special topics such as:

http://memory.loc.gov/ammem/ndlpedu/features/timeline/expref/slavery/slavery.html
Pre–Civil War African-American Slavery.

http://lcweb2.loc.gov/ammem/aaohtml/exhibit/aointro.html
African-American Odyssey site of the Library of Congress, offering special exhibitions.

http://lcweb.loc.gov/exhibits/african/intro.html
The African-American Mosaic Exhibition, a Library of Congress Resource Guide for the Study of Black History and Culture.

http://www.pbs.org/
PBS Online, offering resources related to their programs, including:

http://www.pbs.org/wgbh/aia/home.html
Africans in America.

http://www.pbs.org/weta/thewest/resources/archives/four/
The West, materials for the period 1856 to 1868.

http://odur.let.rug.nl/~usa/D/1826-1850/slavery/fugitxx.htm
Testimony of fugitive slaves.

http://www.ukans.edu/history/VL/USA/ERAS/1850-1860.html
A section of the United States History Index, offering links to information about the years before the Civil War (1850–1960).

http://odur.let.rug.nl/~usa/P/
An index to online materials relating to the Presidents.

http://www.whitehouse.gov/history/presidents/
A section of the White House site offering biographies and images of the Presidents of the United States.

In Print

Your local library will have many books on American history. The following is just a sampling of those relating to this volume.

African American Women: A Biographical Dictionary. Dorothy C. Salem, ed. New York: Garland, 1993.

Berlin, Ira. *Many Thousands Gone*. Cambridge: Harvard, 1998.

Christian, Charles M. *Black Saga*. Boston: Houghton, Mifflin, 1995.

Davis, David Brion. *The Problem of Slavery in Western Culture*. Ithaca: Cornell, 1966.

———. *The Problem of Slavery in the Age of Revolution 1770–1823*. Ithaca: Cornell, 1975.

Dumond, Dwight Lowell. *Anti-Slavery*. Ann Arbor: University of Michigan, 1961.

Foner, Eric. *Free Soil, Free Labor, Free Men*. New York: Oxford, 1970.

Franklin, John Hope. *Racial Equality*. Chicago: University of Chicago, 1976.

Franklin, John Hope, and Alfred Moss, Jr. *From Slavery to Freedom*, 8th ed. New York: Knopf, 2000.

Hine, Darlene Clark, et al., eds. *Black Women in America: An Historical Encyclopedia*. Brooklyn: Carlson, 1993.

Kolchin, Peter. *American Slavery 1619-1877*. New York: Hill & Wang, 1993.

Lutz, Alma. *Crusade for Freedom: Women of the Anti-Slavery Movement*. Boston: Beacon, 1968.

Rawley, James A. *The Trans-Atlantic Slave Trade*. New York: Norton, 1981.

Thomas, Hugh. *The Slave Trade*. New York: Simon & Schuster, 1997.

Walvin, James. *Slavery and the Slave Trade*. Jackson: University Press of Mississippi, 1983.

Note: For other general Internet sites and books, see Vol. 10, starting on p. 82.

Master Index

This Master Index covers all 10 volumes of *The Young Nation* and is repeated at the end of each volume. **Note:** Figures in bold are the volume numbers; the other figures give the page numbers.

A

abolition: See antislavery activities
Acton, Elizabeth 7: 83
Adams, Abigail 2: 39; 3: 64; 7: 9, 12-13, 15, 18, 61; 8: 15; 9: 11
Adams, John 1: 55, 58, 65; 2: 19, 21, 27, 29, 38-44, 46-49, 52; 3: 51, 53, 63-64; 7: 9, 12-13, 15-16, 58; 8: 7, 44; 9: 67; 10: 68
Adams, John Quincy 2: 39; 3: 52, 63-64, 66-67; 4: 23; 5: 12, 28; 7: 12, 17; 9: 67; 10: 68
Adams, Louisa 7: 17
Adams, Samuel 8: 7
Adams-Otis Treaty 3: 42; 4: 78
Adirondack Mountains 3: 15-16
Adventism (Millerism) 9: 80
Africa 3: 6; 6: 25, 28; 8: 40; 9: 49 , 53-54, 73, 85
African Americans 1: 7-8, 22, 26-28, 58, 71, 78, 81-82; 2: 87; 3: 9, 41, 44, 48, 60-61, 68, 78; 4: 69; 5: 7-24, 67, 75, 80; 6: 82; 7: 13, 20, 23; 8: 46-47, 62; 9: 12-13, 18, 25, 41, 51, 53-55, 57-58, 73, 85-86; 10: 10-11, 62-68 (see also slaves and slavery; African Americans, free)
African Americans, free 1: 82, 3: 44, 60-61; 5: 16, 18-21, 26-27, 29-32, 46; 8: 30, 42-43; 9: 18, 85
Agassiz, Elizabeth Cabot Gray 8: 13
Agassiz, Louis 8: 12-13
Aiken, George 9: 40
Akron 7: 27-28
Alabama 1: 41; 2: 86-87; 3: 9, 24-25, 35, 39, 44-46, 48, 52, 54, 55, 68; 5: 12, 31, 34-35, 87; 8: 45; 10: 62
Alamo 3: 77-79, 81
Alaska 1: 14, 87; 3: 11; 4: 15, 18, 45, 84; 6: 65; 10: 67
Albany 1: 24; 3: 15, 17, 19, 26, 29, 30, 76; 6: 35, 52; 8: 17; 10: 24
alcoholic drinks 2: 10-11, 13-15; 6: 72; 7: 39, 80; 8: 75, 77-81
Alcott, Bronson 9: 32
Alcott, Louisa May 9: 32-33
Aldridge, Ira 9: 41
Alexander, Charles 7: 23
Algiers 5: 54-55
Alien and Sedition Acts 2: 6, 12, 15, 21, 39, 42-46, 50-51
Alien Enemies Act 2: 43
Allegheny River 3: 22; 8: 34; 10: 24
Allen, Richard 9: 85-86
Allston, Washington 9: 69
almanacs 8: 22-23, 51-52; 9: 27
alternative communities 7: 58; 8: 75, 85-87; 9: 31, 80-81
Amana Society 9: 81
amendments, constitutional 1: 62, 64, 70-75; 2: 48, 70-71, 75-76; 10: 74-75
American Academy of Arts and Sciences 8: 7, 23
American Anti-Slavery Society 5: 30-31; 7: 21-22, 50
American Association for the Advancement of Science 8: 7, 23
American Fur Company 2: 69; 4: 40; 10: 26
American Party 5: 65
American Philosophical Society 8: 5-6
American Revolution 1: 7-8, 21, 27-29, 33-44, 47, 51, 55-56, 61, 65-66, 68-69, 78, 84, 86-87; 2: 8, 12, 23-27, 35-36, 39, 43, 65-66, 76; 3: 6-7, 12-14, 17, 21, 53; 4: 78-79; 5: 32; 6: 6, 40, 47, 54, 62, 78; 7: 6, 8-13, 29, 67, 87; 8: 5, 44-45; 9: 5, 13, 26-27, 36-37, 40, 67-68, 74-77; 10: 19, 56
American Tract Society 8: 76
Amherst College 9: 18
Amistad 5: 28
Amsterdam 6: 19
Andrews, S. Holmes 10: 1
anesthesia 8: 9, 40-41, 47
Anglicans 1: 24; 9: 75-76
animism 9: 85, 87
Annapolis 1: 21
annexation 4: 13-17, 20-21, 37; 5: 56; 9: 82
Anthony, Susan B. 7: 22-24, 26, 29, 47, 51, 54-56; 8: 79-80
anti-Catholic activities 3: 75; 5: 66; 6: 38-39, 41, 48, 53; 9: 83
anti-Chinese activities 6: 78-83; 10: 61
Anti-Federalists 1: 55-56, 63-64; 2: 7, 21
anti-German activities 5: 66; 6: 70
anti-immigrant activities 2: 39, 42-43; 3: 75; 5: 65-67; 6: 48, 53, 70; 10: 61
anti-Irish activities 2: 42-43; 5: 66
anti-Jewish activities 6: 74
Anti-Masonic Party 3: 75; 5: 65, 67
anti-Mormon activities 4: 70-71, 74-75
Antioch College 9: 17
anti-Scotch-Irish activities 6: 48
antislavery activities 1: 8, 77-78, 82; 2: 5-6, 20; 3: 60, 68, 74; 4: 6, 13, 15, 20, 22-24, 37-38, 69; 5: 10-11, 19, 28-35, 37-38, 40, 43-49, 51, 56, 58-59, 61, 67-73, 77-79, 80-83; 6: 71; 7: 6, 19-27, 41-42, 45, 50, 52-53, 55, 57-58; 8: 44, 75, 80; 9: 18, 24, 31-32, 34, 81, 86
Apaches 4: 77, 82, 84, 86
Apalachicola River 3: 9, 40-41
Appalachian Mountains 1: 7, 19, 21, 26, 28-29, 45-46, 52; 2: 58, 65, 79; 3: 13-15, 20-22, 25; 4: 38, 49; 6: 6, 43, 47; 7: 70; 9: 15, 23, 49, 77; 10: 11, 21, 30
Appert, Nicholas 8: 57
apprentices 8: 42-45, 63; 10: 41
architecture and design 2: 48, 50, 52; 6: 55; 8: 27-34; 9: 62-64
Arista, Mariano 4: 22
Arizona 4: 34, 74, 76-77; 5: 57, 61; 10: 62, 65
Arkansas (people) 3: 54
Arkansas 3: 20, 39, 48, 54, 60, 87; 10: 62
Arkwright, Richard 10: 38, 41, 50
armed forces, U.S. 1: 8, 86; 2: 8, 18, 44, 51-52, 57, 81-82, 85; 3: 7, 34, 38, 40-43, 45-48, 66, 79, 85; 4: 21, 25, 28, 31, 71, 75; 5: 27, 46-47, 80, 87; 7: 11, 38 (see also specific wars)
arms and ammunition 1: 72, 86; 2: 46; 3: 42, 85; 5: 80; 8: 9; 10: 43-44
arms, right to bear 1: 72
Aroostook War 3: 8
Articles of Confederation 1: 44, 57-59
Ashburton, Lord (Alexander Baring) 4: 9
Ashmun Institute 9: 18
Asia 1: 14; 3: 6; 6: 2; 74; 8: 40
Asian Americans 1: 71; 6: 12-13, 29, 82 (see also specific countries)
assassination 5: 77, 85; 7: 18; 9: 38-39
Assiniboine 4: 86
Associated Press 8: 20
Associationism 8: 86-87

Astley, Charles 9: 43
Astor, John Jacob 2: 69; 4: 40; 6: 9; 10: 26
Astoria 2: 68-69
astronomy 8: 7, 22-23
Atkinson, Samuel 9: 23
Atlantic coast 1: 6-7, 21, 23-26, 45, 53; 2: 32, 81; 3: 13-15, 21, 24, 27, 67-68; 4: 38, 45; 5: 14, 35; 6: 27, 33-34, 47, 50, 72; 8: 15, 18; 9: 7, 37; 10: 5-6, 12, 14, 18-20, 30, 42, 45, 51
Atlantic Ocean 1: 11, 19, 53; 2: 30-34, 40-41, 52, 56-57, 72-74, 81, 85; 3: 26, 31; 4: 45; 5: 35; 6: 5, 16-32, 41, 63; 8: 17; 10: 27, 45-47
Attorney General, U.S. 1: 66
Auburn 8: 83-84
Audubon, John James 6: 9; 8: 11-12; 9: 69
Austin, Elizabeth 9: 59
Australia 3: 6; 4: 65
Austria 2: 24, 57, 73; 9: 56

B

Babcock, Alpheus 9: 52
Bache, Sarah Franklin 7: 10
Bad Axe, Battle of 3: 37-38, 48
Bagley, Sarah 7: 42
Bahamas 1: 12
bail, excessive 1: 75
Bailey, Hackaliah 9: 44
ballet and ballerinas 9: 25, 55-56
balloon frame 8: 30-31
balloons, hot-air 8: 20
Baltimore 2: 83-84; 3: 32, 67; 4: 39; 5: 86; 6: 33, 47, 69-70; 8: 19, 37; 9: 37, 64; 10: 14, 19-20
Bank of Pennsylvania 9: 64
Bank of the United States 2: 16-17; 3: 50, 55-57, 65, 72-73
banks 1: 53; 2: 16-17; 3: 50, 55-57, 65, 72-73; 4: 9, 17; 6: 72, 77; 10: 15
Baptists 5: 51; 9: 15, 77-80, 85-86
Barbary Wars 2: 54-55
Barker, James Nelson 9: 40
Barnum, Phineas T. 9: 43, 45, 59-60
Barrymore, Maurice 9: 39
Bartleson party 4: 42
baseball 8: 73
Basques 1: 15; 10: 45
Battery 6: 36, 50
Baum, Martin 6: 72
Bay Path 3: 18
Bear Flag Revolt 4: 30-31
Becknell, William 3: 84
Beecher, Catharine 7: 66; 8: 78; 9: 11, 16-17
Beecher, Lyman 8: 78
Beeton, Isabella 7: 83
Belgian Americans 6: 85; 8: 26
Belknap, Fort 4: 83
Bell, John 5: 86
Bella Coola 4: 19
Bennett, James Gordon 9: 23
Benton, Thomas Hart 4: 40-41, 43
Berea College 9: 18
Bessemer process 10: 44
Best, Jacob 6: 72
Biddle, Nicholas 3: 72-73
Bierstadt, Albert 6: 65; 9: 70
Bigelow, Erastus 8: 8-9
Billings, William 9: 47

bill of attainder 1: 76
Bill of Rights 1: 64, 70-75, 78; 2: 7, 43, 75-76; 6: 41, 74; 7: 29; 9: 10, 74; 10: 74-75
Bingham, George Caleb 4: 15; 5: 37; 9: 70
biology 8: 7, 10-14; 9: 15
Birney, James B. 4: 15
birth 1: 27; 8: 39, 41, 46-49; 10: 9
Bishop, Anna 9: 60
Black Codes 5: 17-18, 27-28
Blackfoot 2: 62; 4: 46, 82-83; 7: 64
Black Hawk (War) 3: 37-38, 48, 84
Blackwell, Antoinette Brown 7: 27-28
Blackwell, Elizabeth 7: 38, 41, 58; 8: 43-44
Blackwell, Henry Brown 7: 38, 58
Bladensburg 2: 84
Blanchard, Jean Pierre 8: 20
Blanchard, Thomas 8: 9
Blatch, Harriot Stanton 7: 45, 47
Blondin 9: 45
Bloomer, Amelia 8: 69, 80; 9: 57
Blue Jacket 2: 37
Blue Mountains 4: 56
boarding houses 6: 21; 7: 87; 10: 52-53
boats: See shipping; steamboats
Bodmer, Karl 2: 62; 4: 40, 84; 8: 10, 28; 9: 70
Bogardus, James 8: 9
Boise, Fort 4: 56
Bonaparte, Napoleon 1: 86; 2: 56-57, 72-73, 83 (see also Napoleonic Wars)
books 9: 7, 9-10, 13, 14, 21-24, 47, 84 (see also literature; libraries; publishing)
Boone, Daniel 1: 7, 29-31, 45; 3: 13, 20; 6: 47
Booth, Edwin 9: 38
Booth, John Wilkes 9: 38-39
Booth, Junius Brutus 9: 38-39
Border Ruffians 5: 70
Boston 1: 35, 40, 83; 2: 39, 80-81; 5: 17-18, 35, 45-47; 6: 33, 48, 76, 86; 7: 2, 9, 19, 30; 8: 7, 12, 17, 30, 39, 43, 57, 74, 76, 78; 9: 7, 10, 20, 31-33, 37-38, 48, 52, 64, 75; 10: 14, 19, 41
Boston Atheneum 9: 20
Boston Female Anti-Slavery Society 7: 2
Boston Handel and Haydn Society 9: 48
Boston Latin School 9: 7
Boston Massacre 1: 35
Boston Public Library 9: 20
Boston Tea Party 1: 35
Boulton, Matthew 10: 39
Bowditch, Nathaniel 8: 22-23
Bowdoin College 5: 29, 53; 9: 18
Bowie, Jim 3: 79
Braddock, Edward 1: 33, 68
Brady, Mathew 8: 21; 9: 60, 72
Brazil 1: 12, 87; 5: 8
Brazilian Americans 6: 75
Breckenridge, John C. 5: 86; 10: 68
Bremen 6: 31
Brest 2: 32
Breton, William L. 10: 11
Bretons 1: 15; 10: 45
bricks 4: 29; 5: 51; 8: 27-28, 30-31
Bridger, Fort 4: 54-55, 72, 75; 5: 62
Bridger, Jim 3: 47; 4: 54
bridges 3: 16, 18; 8: 32-34; 10: 39
Brisbane, Arthur 8: 86-87
Bristow, George Frederick 9: 49, 60
Britain 1: 7-8, 15, 21-28, 32-44, 51-53, 68-69, 72, 78-79, 81-82, 84-87; 2: 18, 23-34, 39-41, 49, 55, 57, 59, 62-63, 69, 72-74, 77-85; 3: 6-8, 13, 14, 24, 32, 34-35, 37, 62, 64, 68,

77; **4:** 9, 11-13, 15-16, 18-19, 42-43, 78; **5:** 8, 10-11, 23-24, 27, 74; **6:** 7, 9, 25, 38-39, 42, 44, 46, 62, 78-79, 86; **7:** 6, 10-13, 17, 20, 30, 32, 67; **8:** 6, 12, 25, 33, 41, 43, 65, 76, 82; **9:** 5, 7, 13, 17, 20, 25, 27-29, 34, 36-41, 43, 59, 61-64, 67-68, 74-76, 83; **10:** 5, 7, 11, 19, 21, 33-34, 36-40, 45, 47, 49-50, 54
British Americans **1:** 7; **6:** 7, 9-10, 12-13, 17, 20-22, 31, 33, 35, 54-60; **9:** 25, 46-47, 49, 73, 80; **10:** 40-41 (see also colonies, American)
British-American Convention of 1818 **2:** 69; **3:** 8; **4:** 18
British East India Company **1:** 52; **4:** 12; **6:** 79
Brook Farm **8:** 87
Brooklyn **8:** 30, 34; **9:** 60; **10:** 17
Brown (Blackwell), Antoinette **7:** 27-28
Brown, Charles Brockden **7:** 36, 58; **9:** 27
Brown, James **9:** 41
Brown, John **5:** 6, 20, 25, 38, 71, 74, 80-82
Brown, John Henry **5:** 84
Brown, Joshua **9:** 44
Brown, Moses **10:** 41
Brown, William Hill **9:** 27
Brown University **9:** 13
Bryant, William Cullen **9:** 26, 33, 69
bubble, financial **3:** 55, 57, 72-73
Buchanan, James **5:** 53, 73-74, 76; **6:** 48; **7:** 17-18; **10:** 68
Buena Vista **4:** 25-27, 31; **5:** 39
Buffalo **3:** 15-17, 19, 26-29; **6:** 52; **9:** 81; **10:** 14-15, 21, 23
buffalo **2:** 62; **4:** 51, 63
building and construction **5:** 21; **6:** 51-52, 58; **8:** 9, 17, 27-34; **10:** 56
Bulfinch, Charles **9:** 62-65
Burden, Henry **8:** 9
Burgoyne, John **1:** 41
Burlington, Richard **9:** 62
Burns, Anthony **5:** 45, 47
Burr, Aaron **2:** 12, 38, 47-48, 51-52, 70-71; **10:** 68
Burr, Theodore **8:** 33
Bushnell, E. W. **8:** 74
business and finance **1:** 51-53, 66; **2:** 7-12, 16-17, 19, 50, 71; **3:** 49, 51; **4:** 9; **5:** 21; **6:** 8-9, 71-72, 74-77; **7:** 30, 32, 42, 61, 64, 71-72, 80, 84-87; **8:** 87; **9:** 17; **10:** 15, 30
Butterfield Stage **5:** 61-62; **8:** 18

C

Cabinet, President's **1:** 61, 66; **2:** 51-52; **3:** 65; **4:** 9-10
Cabot, John **1:** 15
Cabral, Pedro **1:** 12
Cabrillo, Juan **1:** 16
Caddos **3:** 81
Cádiz **2:** 73
Caldwell, James **9:** 40
Caldwell, John **9:** 60
Calhoun, John C. **3:** 63, 69-70; **4:** 13, 23
California **1:** 7, 16-18, 86-87; **3:** 77, 82, 86-87; **4:** 5, 15-16, 18, 20-21, 28-31, 34, 36-37, 39, 42-44, 47-48, 51, 56-57, 60-69, 71, 76-79, 86-87; **5:** 23, 37, 43, 60-63, 73; **6:** 29, 50, 53, 66-67, 78, 80-83, 87; **7:** 34; **8:** 20, 73; **9:** 30, 51, 60, 83, 87; **10:** 7, 10, 48, 62
California Trail **4:** 5, 42, 44, 55, 60-63, 67; **5:** 62-63
Calvinists **6:** 62
Cambridge **1:** 35; **9:** 13
Camino Real, El **1:** 17, 87
camp meetings **7:** 26; **9:** 74, 77-79
Campbell, Colen **9:** 62
Canada **1:** 7, 15, 21, 33, 37, 43, 78, 86-87; **2:** 58-59, 63, 73, 79-83; **3:** 6-8, 62; **4:** 9, 11, 18-19, 42, 45, 81, 84; **5:** 32, 34-35, 47; **6:** 7, 25, 31-32, 40-41, 43, 46, 54-55, 59-60; **8:** 87; **10:** 6
Canadian Americans **6:** 7, 10, 12, 17, 31, 33, 35, 40, 43, 50, 54, 59-60, 85
canals **1:** 83; **3:** 12, 16-18, 26-33; **4:** 35-36; **6:** 5, 10, 19, 34-35, 49, 52; **8:** 15-17, 34; **9:** 37, 44-45; **10:** 9, 12, 15-16, 18, 23-24
Cane Ridge **9:** 78-79
canning and meatpacking **4:** 58; **8:** 57-58; **10:** 30, 44
canoes **1:** 20; **3:** 10, 19; **8:** 11
Canton **4:** 12, 29; **6:** 80, 82
Cape Horn **1:** 52; **4:** 63, 65
capital, U.S. **1:** 65-67; **2:** 7, 16, 47-48; **5:** 14, 43, 64; **6:** 7; **7:** 12, 15-16; **10:** 18
Capitol, U.S. **2:** 48-49, 84; **3:** 61, 72; **4:** 5; **5:** 52, 83; **6:** 55, 85; **9:** 20, 62-65, 71
Caribbean **1:** 12-13, 41, 53; **2:** 12, 30-32, 40-41, 51-52, 57, 59, 72-74, 81; **3:** 10, 62; **4:** 15; **5:** 7-9, 32, 35, 56; **6:** 12, 25, 27; **9:** 13, 25, 49, 54, 73; **10:** 27-28
Carnegie, Andrew **6:** 54
Carolinas **3:** 20, 25; **5:** 13, 34; **6:** 62; **7:** 62; **9:** 75; **10:** 20
Caroline, Fort **1:** 16
Carroll, John **9:** 82
Carson, Kit **3:** 87
Cartier, Jacques **1:** 15, 19
Cartwright, Alexander **8:** 73
Cass, Lewis **5:** 39, 41, 53, 59; **10:** 68
Castle Garden **6:** 36-37, 52-53
Catholics **1:** 18-19, 21, 25, 87; **2:** 24, 42; **4:** 69; **5:** 66; **6:** 7, 34, 38-41-42, 48-53, 67; **9:** 14-15, 47, 64, 73, 82-83, 87
Catlin, George **3:** 40, 47, 81, 83, 85-86; **7:** 61; **9:** 70
Catskill Mountains **3:** 15-16; **9:** 70
Cayley, George **8:** 20
Cayugas **3:** 14
Cayuses **3:** 86
census, U.S. **1:** 79, 81; **6:** 16; **9:** 10, 12, 72; **10:** 8, 10, 62-67
Central America **1:** 12-13, 87; **4:** 15, 63; **5:** 56-57; **6:** 80
Central Americans **6:** 12-13
Cerro Gordo **4:** 32
Champlain, Lake **2:** 84; **3:** 6
Champlain, Samuel de **1:** 21
Chandler School **9:** 16
Channing, William Ellery **7:** 20
Chapman, Maria Weston **7:** 20, 22
Chapultepec Hill **4:** 33
Charleston **1:** 26; **5:** 25-27, 86-87; **6:** 33, 75; **7:** 25; **8:** 74; **9:** 36, 38, 48, 55-56; **10:** 20
Charlestown (MA) **6:** 48
Charlestown (VA) **5:** 82
Chase, Salmon P. **5:** 86
checks and balances **1:** 60
chemistry **8:** 6-7, 10, 36, 44
Cherokee Nation v. Georgia **3:** 46
Cherokees **1:** 29-30, 87; **2:** 36, 87; **3:** 39, 44, 46-48, 65, 76, 80-81; **9:** 40
Chesapeake **2:** 74
Chesapeake Bay **1:** 42; **5:** 23; **10:** 20
Cheyenne **4:** 85
Cheyney University of Pennsylvania **9:** 18
Chicago **2:** 18; **3:** 17, 35, 57; **5:** 86; **6:** 25, 52, 66, 70; **8:** 31, 57; **10:** 14, 21, 25-26
Chicago Turnpike **3:** 17, 21
Chickasaws **2:** 36; **3:** 20-21, 39, 45
Chickasaw Trail **3:** 20-21
Chickering, Jonas **9:** 52
Chihuahua (Trail) **3:** 82-84; **4:** 31
Child, Francis J. **9:** 47
Child, Lydia Maria **7:** 19, 23, 51, 65-66; **8:** 70-71
child labor **8:** 52, 54, 64; **9:** 10; **10:** 50-53, 55, 58
children **3:** 14, 58, 78; **5:** 7, 9, 15, 20-22; **6:** 11; **7:** 22, 27, 36-37, 56, 59-60, 63-64, 67, 72, 78; **8:** 36, 46-49, 51, 62-64; **9:** 6-12 (see also child labor)
China **1:** 52, 87; **2:** 31; **3:** 6; **4:** 11-12; **5:** 54-55; **6:** 53, 78-83; **9:** 63; **10:** 19
Chinese Americans **4:** 66, 69; **6:** 12, 29, 78-83, 85
Chinese Exclusion Act **6:** 83
Choctaws **2:** 36; **3:** 39, 44-45, 48
cholera **4:** 63, 84; **6:** 29; **8:** 38-39, 49
Christians and Christianity **1:** 9, 23; **4:** 70; **5:** 48; **6:** 74; **8:** 76; **9:** 57, 73-83, 85-87 (see also specific groups)
Christina, Fort **1:** 24
Christmas **8:** 71; **9:** 47-48
Church of England in the Colonies **9:** 75, 77
Church of Jesus Christ of Latter-day Saints: See Mormons
Church, Frederic Edwin **9:** 70
Churubusco **4:** 33
cider **7:** 79; **8:** 58, 77, 81
Cincinnati **2:** 42; **6:** 34, 52, 63, 66, 69-70; **7:** 24, 54, 54; **8:** 57, 73; **9:** 16, 84; **10:** 14, 21, 25
circuses **9:** 43-45
cities and towns **1:** 12, 47, 83; **6:** 49-52; **7:** 60, 64-65, 71, 74, 77, 84, 87; **8:** 22, 30-32, 34-36, 46-47, 50, 53-54, 59-61; **9:** 11, 21, 37, 57, 78-79; **10:** 5-6, 9, 11-12, 14-26, 30, 62-68 (see also specific cities)
citizenship **2:** 18, 42-43; **5:** 76; **6:** 74, 83; **9:** 5, 37
civil disobedience **4:** 23; **9:** 32
Civil War, American **1:** 7, 37, 50, 59, 77, 82; **2:** 6; **3:** 10, 28, 33, 38, 49, 58, 60, 70, 74; **4:** 5, 10, 24, 36-37, 39, 56, 58, 63, 69, 82, 85; **5:** 6-7, 11, 16, 18-20, 34-38, 43-44, 46-47, 60-62, 74-75, 77, 80, 81-83, 85, 87; **6:** 71; **7:** 25, 84, 86; **8:** 16, 18, 45; **9:** 11, 16, 42, 53, 72; **10:** 17, 20, 34, 43, 61
Clark, Billy J. **8:** 78
Clark, William **2:** 67-69; **4:** 40
Clay, Cassius M. **9:** 18
Clay, Henry **3:** 60, 63, 70-72, 75; **4:** 13, 15, 38; **5:** 41-43; **10:** 68
Clemens, Samuel Langhorne **9:** 33-34
Clermont **3:** 20; **8:** 17
Cleveland **6:** 52
Clinch, Charles **9:** 40
Clinton, DeWitt **3:** 26, 33; **10:** 9, 68
Clinton, George **2:** 21, 70, 75
clothing and cloth **1:** 52; **5:** 33; **6:** 24; **7:** 10-11, 59, 61, 63, 65, 67-73; **10:** 38-39, 44
coal **6:** 57; **8:** 26, 36-37; **10:** 23, 37
Coercive Acts **1:** 35, 72
Coffin, Catherine **5:** 32
Coffin, Levi **5:** 32
Cohens v. Virginia **3:** 51
Cole, Thomas **5:** 35; **9:** 67, 69-70
College of Physicians and Surgeons **8:** 43
colleges and universities **7:** 13; **8:** 11, 43-44, 73-74; **9:** 5-6, 11, 13-19
colonies, American **1:** 6-7, 14-27, 32-35, 37, 84-85; **3:** 9, 14, 77-78, 82; **4:** 78-79; **5:** 7-8, 10, 17, 29; **6:** 7, 22-24, 34, 38-39, 48, 54-56, 62, 68-69, 75, 86; **7:** 9, 12; **8:** 25, 30, 59, 65, 73-74, 82; **9:** 6-7, 13-14, 19, 26-27, 36-37, 46-48, 55, 57, 59, 66, 73-74, 80, 84; **10:** 19, 20, 30-31, 35, 40-41, 56 (see also specific colonies)
Colorado **2:** 69; **4:** 34, 74; **5:** 38; **10:** 62, 65
Colt, Samuel **8:** 9
Columbia River **2:** 68; **4:** 19, 46, 56, 58
Columbia University **2:** 12; **9:** 13
Columbus, Christopher **1:** 9-10, 12-13, 25
Comanches **1:** 8; **3:** 79, 81-83; **5:** 47; **7:** 61
Committees of Correspondence **2:** 52
Committees of Public Safety **2:** 14
communications **8:** 15, 17-21 (see also letters; telegraph; newspapers)
company towns **10:** 51-52
Compromise of 1850 **5:** 6, 15, 38, 42-44, 52, 64
Concepción **3:** 78
Concord **1:** 35-36, 40; **9:** 31
Confederate States of America **3:** 38; **4:** 10, 39; **5:** 80, 87; **9:** 42
Confederation of the United States of America **1:** 43-56, 59, 65, 67-69, 79, 82; **2:** 36, 76; **7:** 8, 34
Congregationalists **7:** 27-28; **9:** 15, 75-77, 79
Congress, U.S. **1:** 56, 59-62, 65-67, 70; **2:** 5-6, 10-11, 13, 16-17, 19, 41-44, 47-49, 51, 76, 79-80; **3:** 36, 50-51, 54, 58, 60-62, 69, 72, 80; **4:** 10, 13, 16-17, 20, 22-24, 65, 69, 74, 79; **5:** 29, 37, 42-43, 58-59, 61, 72, 75, 84; **7:** 8, 25, 28; **8:** 19; **9:** 63
Connecticut **1:** 64, 82, 84; **2:** 11, 79; **3:** 12; **5:** 45-46; **8:** 25, 78; **9:** 12, 32, 65; **10:** 12, 17, 62
conscription **2:** 18, 24
Constitution **2:** 41, 80-81
Constitution, U.S. **1:** 44, 47, 55-65, 67, 70-79, 84; **2:** 6-7, 12, 19, 47-48, 53, 70, 75-76; **3:** 46, 50-51, 58; **5:** 6, 67; **6:** 41, 74; **7:** 8-9, 29; **8:** 72; **9:** 74, 76; **10:** 18, 69-75
Constitution, U.S., ratification of **1:** 63-64, 84-85; **8:** 72
Constitutional Convention **1:** 54-62, 69; **2:** 12, 76
Constitutional Union Party **5:** 86
Constitution Day **8:** 72
Continental Army **1:** 33, 61, 69; **2:** 24; **7:** 9, 11; **8:** 44
Continental Congress **1:** 37, 44, 84; **2:** 39, 52; **3:** 53; **7:** 11-13
Continental Divide **2:** 68; **4:** 45-46
Contreras **4:** 33
Cooke, George Frederick **9:** 38
cooking **6:** 15, 72; **7:** 10, 20, 24, 62, 78-83, 85; **8:** 9, 28
cooling and refrigeration **7:** 63, 79; **8:** 56
Cooper, James Fenimore **8:** 68; **9:** 26, 28, 40
Cooper, Peter **3:** 32; **8:** 8-9, 17
Cooper, Thomas Abthorpe **9:** 37-38
Cooper Union **5:** 83; **8:** 8-9
Copley, John Singleton **9:** 67
Copyright Act **2:** 19
Corbin, Margaret Cochran **7:** 11
Cornish Americans **6:** 7, 54, 57-58
Cornwall (Britain) **6:** 7
Cornwall (CT) **6:** 78
Cornwallis, Charles **1:** 42, 69
Coronado, Francisco Vásquez de **1:** 16
Corpus Christi **4:** 21
Costa Rica **5:** 57
cotton **1:** 23, 53; **3:** 12, 24-25, 56, 58, 68, 78; **4:** 38; **5:** 5, 13-14, 17, 34; **6:** 9, 13, 24, 56-57, 69; **7:** 67-69, 78; **8:** 51, 53, 66; **10:** 10, 20-22, 29-30, 33-35, 37, 39, 41-42, 44, 49, 52
cotton gin **3:** 24; **5:** 5, 13; **7:** 68; **10:** 31, 33-34, 37, 39, 44
Council Grove **3:** 84
coverture **7:** 33
Crandall, Prudence **9:** 12
Crawford, William **9:** 71
Crawford, William H. **3:** 63
credit, financial **1:** 48, 53; **3:** 55-57, 65, 72-73; **4:** 16-17
Creek-American War **2:** 86-87; **3:** 35, 39, 40, 48, 66, 77, 80
Creeks **2:** 36, 86-87; **3:** 35, 39, 40-41, 45, 48, 66, 77, 80, 87; **5:** 23
Crockett, Davy **3:** 79
crops **8:** 51-58; **10:** 5, 21, 27, 29-30, 33-35 (see also grain)
Cropsey, Jasper **9:** 70
Crows **4:** 84, 86
Crystal Palace **8:** 32
Cuba **4:** 15; **5:** 28, 56-57
Cumberland Gap **1:** 7, 28, 30, 45-46; **2:** 65; **3:** 13, 20-21; **6:** 47, 69

Cumberland River 3: 16, 20
Cumberland Road 3: 23
Currency Act 1: 34
Cushing, Caleb 4: 11-12
Cushman, Charlotte 9: 39

D

Daguerre, Louis 9: 72
daguerreotypes 4: 23; 9: 60, 72
dairy products 7: 60, 78-80; 8: 55, 57, 67; 10: 30
Dakotas 9: 54, 87
Dakota Territory 4: 84, 86; 10: 65
Dallas 4: 76
Dana, James Dwight 8: 13-14
Dana, Richard Henry 9: 30
dance and dancers 7: 18; 8: 58; 9: 11, 24-25, 53-58, 80
Dancing Rabbit Creek, Treaty of 3: 45
Danish Americans 6: 12, 19, 35, 86-87
dark horse candidate 4: 16-17; 5: 53
Dartmouth College 9: 13-14, 16
Dartmouth College v. Woodward 9: 14
Daughters of Liberty 7: 10
Davis, Alexander Jackson 9: 65
Davis, Jefferson 3: 38; 5: 87
Davis, John 9: 60
Davis, Paulina Wright 7: 54-55
Davis, Samuel Luther 8: 7
Day, Benjamin 9: 23
Dearborn, Fort 2: 18, 33, 81; 3: 35
death: See disease and death
debts and debtors 2: 8, 11, 51; 3: 55-57; 6: 22-23, 29; 7: 42; 8: 82; 10: 59
Decatur, Stephen 2: 54-55
Declaration of Independence 1: 34, 37-39, 55, 57-59, 66, 76, 78; 2: 23, 38-39, 44, 52; 3: 53; 4: 8; 7: 9, 12-13, 29, 46; 8: 44, 72; 9: 26, 62; 10: 18
Declaration of Sentiments and Resolutions 4: 17; 7: 32, 43, 45-49, 51, 57-58
Declaration of the Rights of Man and Citizen 2: 23, 25; 7: 29
Declaration of the Rights of Woman and Citizen 7: 32
Deere, John 10: 32
Delaware 1: 64, 82, 84; 6: 86; 10: 62
Delaware River 1: 24, 41; 8: 17
Delawares 3: 37, 48; 4: 48
Democratic-Republicans 2: 20; 3: 52, 64, 71; 5: 69; 10: 68
Democrats 2: 20; 3: 71, 75; 4: 8-10, 13-17; 5: 37, 39-41, 52-53, 59, 64, 68-69, 73-74, 76, 78, 83, 86; 10: 59, 68
dentistry and dental care 7: 85; 8: 9, 41, 45
deportation 2: 43
depression, economic 1: 53, 79; 3: 33, 53, 56, 73, 75-76; 6: 6, 13; 10: 49, 57
Derham, James 8: 42-43
Deseret 4: 74
Deslandes, Charles 5: 26
de Soto, Hernando 1: 16
Dessalines, John-Jacques 5: 24
Detroit 2: 81-82; 3: 17; 10: 21
Dial, The 7: 30-31; 9: 31
Dickens, Charles 10: 54
Dickinson, Anna Elizabeth 7: 25
Dickinson, Emily 9: 35
disease and death 1: 12-13, 15-16, 18, 26-27; 2: 71; 3: 47-48, 86; 4: 6, 8, 49, 63, 84; 5: 8-9, 18, 48, 58; 6: 14-15, 28-29, 43, 45-46; 7: 17; 8: 38-47, 49, 63, 76-77, 87; 9: 34, 87; 10: 9, 11, 19
disestablishment 9: 76
dissenters, religious 1: 24; 6: 62
divorce 7: 32, 35, 37-40, 56, 59; 8: 79
Dix, Dorothea 7: 31; 8: 45
Doak's Stand, Treaty of 3: 44
doctors: See physicians

Dominican Republic 1: 12
Doniphan, Alexander 4: 31
Donner Party 4: 61-62
double jeopardy 1: 73
Douglas, Stephen 5: 52, 58-60, 77-79, 85-86
Douglass, David 9: 36
Douglass, Frederick 5: 19-20, 31; 7: 45-46, 57-58
dower rights 7: 35
Dragging Canoe 1: 30
Drake, Samuel 9: 42
Dred Scott decision 3: 74; 5: 6, 38, 74-76, 79
dress, fashions in 7: 11, 15, 71-73; 8: 65-69, 81
Drew, Georgianna 9: 39
Drew, John 9: 39
Drew, Louisa Lane 9: 39
Duden, Gottfried 6: 66
due process of law 1: 73
Duluth, Daniel 1: 21
Dunlap, William 9: 40, 70
Duquesne, Fort 1: 32-33; 10: 24
Durand, Asher B. 9: 69-70
Durang, John 9: 55
Dutch Americans 6: 12, 19, 85; 8: 71; 9: 28 (see also Netherlands)

E

East and Easterners 3: 72; 4: 38, 65; 7: 34, 73
East Asia 2: 74
East Coast: See Atlantic coast
East Indies 1: 12, 24
Eastman, Seth 7: 72; 9: 54, 87
education 5: 19, 21, 29, 51; 6: 71, 78; 7: 13, 23, 42, 59, 66, 85; 8: 13-14, 54, 75; 9: 5-18, 21, 24, 32, 81; 10: 51, 59
education, for African Americans 5: 21; 9: 12, 18
education, for Native Americans 9: 12, 14, 18
education, for women 7: 27, 30-32, 38, 41-42, 66, 85-86; 8: 13, 43-46; 9: 10-13, 16-18
Egypt 2: 55, 57; 9: 63
Einhorn, David 9: 84
elections, congressional 1: 59-61; 5: 69, 79; 7: 5, 7
elections, presidential 1: 61; 2: 21-22, 38-39, 47-48, 70-71; 3: 52, 63-64, 66, 71, 75-76; 4: 6-10, 14-17; 5: 37, 39-41, 52-53, 73-74, 83-86; 7: 5, 7; 10: 68
Electoral College 1: 61, 65; 2: 21; 4: 15
electricity 8: 5, 9, 18-19, 26, 37; 10: 46
elevator 8: 32
Elliott, Charles Loring 10: 31
Ellis Island 6: 36-37
El Morro 4: 50
El Paso 1: 17; 4: 31, 76; 5: 61
El Salvador 5: 57
Elssler, Fanny 9: 56
Emancipation Proclamation 1: 23; 2: 6; 5: 85
Embargo Act 2: 74
Emerson, Ralph Waldo 1: 36; 8: 10, 87; 9: 26, 31
emigration in North America 1: 6-8, 25-26, 28-31, 45-50, 78-79, 83; 2: 6, 33-36, 50, 57, 60-69, 83, 86; 3: 5, 9, 12-35, 42-44, 47, 49, 55, 65, 75, 77-78, 86-87; 4: 5, 11, 13-86; 5: 13, 37-38, 56-59, 86; 6: 5, 8, 34; 7: 69-70; 8: 49, 67; 9: 5, 16, 37, 42, 51, 69, 78-79; 10: 11-17, 21-26, 29, 36
Emmett, Daniel Decatur 9: 42
engineering 8: 7, 9, 9: 63-64
England: See Britain
English Channel 2: 57; 6: 19
Enlightenment 8: 82
Episcopal Church 9: 77
Ericsson, John 8: 9
Erie, Fort 2: 83
Erie, Lake 2: 79, 82; 3: 17, 26, 28; 10: 23
Erie Canal 3: 16-18, 26-29, 33; 4: 35; 6: 5, 10, 34-35, 49, 52, 64, 69; 9: 37, 44-45; 10: 9, 12, 15-16, 18, 23-24

Erik the Red 1: 14
ethnic cleansing 3: 36
Europe 1: 9-33, 86-87; 2: 23-26, 41, 51, 54-57, 59, 62, 72-74, 79; 3: 6, 21, 24, 27, 34, 62, 67-68; 4: 81; 5: 8, 11, 23, 54-55; 6: 6-8, 10-11, 25, 27, 39, 44, 63, 66, 74-76, 79, 84-85; 7: 14, 30; 8: 21, 25, 28, 32, 35-36, 40-42, 65-66, 82, 85; 9: 10, 25, 27, 31, 38, 43, 45-48, 52, 54-56, 65, 71, 73, 76, 83; 10: 21, 27-28, 36, 45, 49 (see also specific countries)
European Americans 3: 17, 26-27; 4: 35, 38; 5: 9; 6: 10-14, 17-19, 21-32, 84-87; 10: 9, 13, 16 (see also specific countries; colonies, American)
Evans, Oliver 8: 17, 25-26; 10: 28
Everglades 3: 43
executive branch 1: 60-61, 66
ex post facto law 1: 76
expulsions, Native-American 1: 8, 15, 26, 29, 31, 46; 2: 36-37, 66, 77-78, 86-87; 3: 34-48, 65-66, 68, 78; 4: 48, 81-87; 6: 6; 9: 87; 10: 10-11, 29
extraterritoriality, principle of 4: 12

F

Fallen Timbers, Battle of 2: 37
Fall Line Road 3: 25
Fall River 6: 28, 57
families 3: 13; 7: 63, 72, 76-77; 8: 62-64, 77; 10: 9, 50, 52
Far East 2: 31
farm machinery 8: 9, 63; 10: 28, 31-32, 43
farms and farmers 1: 29, 48, 51, 53-54, 83, 86; 2: 13-15, 72, 79; 3: 12-14, 17, 24, 36, 55-56, 68; 4: 16-17, 36, 38-39, 49, 58, 68; 5: 12, 16, 21; 6: 6, 8, 11, 13-16, 34, 42, 44-46, 47, 53, 59-60, 62, 64-65, 68-69, 72, 74, 76, 83, 87; 7: 59-60, 63, 65, 67-70, 78-79; 8: 7, 10, 24, 26, 37, 56-68; 9: 57, 78; 10: 5, 9, 14, 23, 27, 29-35, 62-68
federal government, U.S. 1: 37, 47, 54-56, 59-67, 70-71, 77; 2: 6-11, 13-19, 21, 42-48, 51, 53, 74; 3: 23, 25, 45, 49-51, 56-57, 68-69, 70, 74; 4: 9, 75; 6: 23; 10: 44, 58
Federal Hall 1: 27, 65-67
Federalists 1: 55-56, 65; 2: 7, 9, 12, 15, 17, 19, 29, 38-39, 43-52, 70, 75, 79; 3: 68; 8: 78-79; 9: 27; 10: 68
Federal Reserve 2: 17
Federal Road 3: 25
Fee, John G. 9: 18
Female Anti-Slavery Society 7: 20
feme sole 7: 35
ferries 3: 18; 4: 48, 56, 72; 6: 19; 8: 32
54-40 or fight 4: 19, 43
filibusters 5: 56-57
Fillmore, Millard 5: 40-42, 52, 64, 67, 74; 10: 68
fines, excessive 1: 75
Finley, James 8: 33
Finney, Charles Grandison 9: 79
Finnish Americans 6: 86-87; 9: 79
First Ladies 7: 12, 14-19
Fisher, Alanson 9: 33
fishing 1: 15, 31; 2: 31; 4: 18, 58-59, 68, 83; 6: 82-83; 7: 81; 8: 54, 57; 10: 20, 45-46
Fitch, John 8: 17
flag, U.S. 3: 76; 7: 8
flax 6: 24; 7: 67-69; 8: 53; 10: 30
Fletcher v. Peck 2: 53
flight 8: 20
Florence 1: 10; 9: 71
Florida 1: 9, 15-17, 42-43, 87; 2: 29, 34-35, 57, 63, 78; 3: 9, 40-44, 48, 65-66, 77; 4: 37, 39, 78; 5: 11, 22-23, 25, 33, 35, 87; 9: 87; 10: 6, 63
folk art 8: 48; 9: 58, 66
folk dancing 9: 57-58
folk music 9: 46-48, 85

food 2: 30-31, 72; 3: 14, 17, 18, 45, 47; 5: 33; 6: 15, 21-22, 24-26, 28, 44-46, 65, 72; 7: 10, 59, 62-63, 65, 78-83; 8: 51-58; 9: 17; 10: 15, 19-20, 27, 29-30
food preservation 7: 63, 79-80; 8: 54, 56-58
Force Act 3: 70
Forrest, Edwin 9: 39-40
Fort Lee 8: 20
Fort Wayne 2: 37
Fort Worth 4: 76
Forty-Eighters 6: 67
Forty-Niners 4: 65, 68, 76-77, 85; 10: 48
49th parallel 3: 8; 4: 19
Fosdick, William Whiteman 9: 53
fossils 8: 6, 13
Foster, Stephen 9: 42, 50-51, 53
Fourier, Charles 8: 85-87
Fourth of July 8: 50, 72; 9: 52; 10: 18
Fowler, Lydia 8: 44
Fox 3: 37-38, 48
France 1: 15-16, 19-22, 25, 28, 32-33, 41-42, 44, 53, 68, 79, 81-82, 85-86; 2: 12, 22-32, 34, 39-41, 46, 51-52, 55-59, 62, 67, 72-73, 76, 78; 3: 6, 10, 14, 62, 77-78; 5: 23-24, 49; 6: 7, 84; 8: 65, 86; 9: 25, 34, 38, 55, 60, 72, 87; 10: 6, 24, 47
Francisqui, Jean-Baptiste 9: 55-56
Franklin, Benjamin 1: 37, 43-44, 54-55, 58, 66; 2: 5-6, 23; 5: 29; 7: 9-10, 83; 8: 5, 36; 9: 7, 19, 27
Franklin stove 8: 5, 36
Free Soil Party 4: 6; 5: 40, 53
Free State Party 5: 71-72, 81
free states 1: 60, 82; 3: 54, 58; 4: 37-38, 59, 69, 78-79; 5: 37-38, 40, 43, 50, 58-59, 70-72, 75-76, 79
Frémont, Jessie Benton 4: 41-43
Frémont, John Charles 4: 21, 29-31, 41-43, 68-69, 73-74; 10: 68
French Americans 2: 43; 6: 7, 9, 12, 19, 84; 8: 45; 9: 47, 49, 55, 73, 82-83
French and Indian War 1: 32-34, 68; 2: 59; 3: 10, 14; 4: 78-79
French Canadians 6: 59-60
French Revolution 1: 86; 2: 19, 21-27, 34, 39, 41, 43, 51, 56; 6: 63; 7: 29, 32; 8: 6
Freneau, Philip 2: 19; 9: 27
frontier and frontier people 1: 45, 77; 2: 13-15, 18, 37, 58, 69; 3: 10, 17, 66, 79, 87; 4: 36, 54, 57; 5: 84; 6: 47-48, 62, 87; 7: 7, 13, 60, 67-73, 75, 85; 8: 35, 46-47, 67-69, 81; 9: 7, 11, 16, 28, 42, 51, 57, 77-78, 81; 10: 22
Fugitive Slave Act 5: 6, 38, 44-48
Fuller, Margaret 7: 30-32; 8: 87; 9: 31
Fulton, Robert 3: 30; 8: 17
fund-raising 7: 10, 20, 23-24
furnishings and decorations 7: 15-16, 18, 66; 8: 28-29, 54, 59; 9: 66

G

Gadsden Purchase 5: 56-57; 10: 7
Gage, Matilda 7: 47
Gama, Vasco da 1: 10
Gandhi, Mohandas (Mahatma) 9: 32
García, Manuel 9: 59
García, Maria Felicita 9: 59
Gardette, James 8: 45
Garrison, William Lloyd 3: 68; 5: 28-29, 51; 7: 21-22, 24, 55, 58
gas 7: 77; 8: 36-37
Genet, Edmond 2: 29
genocide 3: 36; 4: 87; 10: 10
geology 8: 6-7, 10, 12-14
Georgetown 2: 10; 5: 64
Georgetown University 9: 14
Georgia 1: 7, 28, 46, 64, 82, 84; 2: 65, 86-87; 3: 24-25, 35, 39, 40, 46, 48, 55, 68-69; 5: 12, 34, 47, 87; 6: 33, 62, 75; 7: 65; 8: 15; 9: 14; 10: 13, 20, 63

Georgia (Wesleyan) Female College **9**: 17

German Americans **2**: 42; **4**: 5; **6**: 7, 9-10, 12-15, 18-19, 22, 30, 34-35, 56, 61-72, 75-76; **8**: 71-72; **9**: 25, 28, 46-49, 52, 70, 79-81; **10**: 16, 20

Germany **1**: 25, 81-82; **2**: 42; **6**: 7, 44; **8**: 37; **9**: 16, 24-25, 49, 84

Geronimo **4**: 86

Ghent, Treaty of **2**: 84; **3**: 35, 64

Ghost Dance movement **9**: 87

Gibbons v. Ogden **3**: 51

Godey, Louis **9**: 24

Godey's Lady's Book **7**: 66; **8**: 66; **9**: 23-24

Godwin, William **7**: 31

gold **1**: 7; **3**: 72-73; **4**: 5, 36, 39, 57, 59, 62-69, 78; **6**: 29, 50, 52-53, 66-67, 78, 80-83, 87; **7**: 34; **8**: 73; **9**: 51, 60; **10**: 14

Goodyear, Charles **8**: 9

Gothic Revival **9**: 65

Gottschalk, Louis Moreau **9**: 49, 53

Gouges, Olympe de **7**: 32

grain **2**: 13, 31; **3**: 34; **6**: 24; **7**: 78, 81-82; **8**: 51, 53, 55, 58, 81; **10**: 5, 19-20, 23, 29-30, 35

Gratz, Rebecca **6**: 74

Gray, Asa **8**: 13

Great Dismal Swamp **5**: 23

Great Lakes **1**: 21; **3**: 6-8, 12, 17, 28; **6**: 34, 64; **8**: 26; **10**: 15, 23, 26

Great Medicine Road **4**: 44

Great Valley Road **3**: 25

Greece **9**: 62-63

Greek Americans **6**: 85

Greek Revival **9**: 63-65

Greeley, Horace **4**: 23-24; **7**: 31; **8**: 86; **9**: 23

Green Bay **6**: 61; **8**: 26

Greenland **1**: 14

Greenough, Horatio **9**: 71

Greenville Treaty **2**: 37

Greenwood, John **8**: 45

Gregg, Josiah (dentist) **8**: 45

Gregg, Josiah (writer) **3**: 84-85

Grimaldi, Joey **9**: 45

Grimké, Angelina **7**: 21, 24-25

Grimké, Sarah **7**: 21, 24-25, 42

Guadalupe Hidalgo, Treaty of **4**: 34, 62, 64, 78; **5**: 56-57; **9**: 82-83

Guangzhou **4**: 12, 29; **6**: 80, 82

Guatemala **5**: 57

Guerrière **2**: 80-81

Gulf Coast **1**: 43, 87; **2**: 29, 34, 57, 64, 85; **3**: 9; **6**: 27, 34, 72; **10**: 6

Gulf Stream **6**: 25

Guthrie, Samuel **8**: 40

H

habeas corpus, writ of **1**: 76

Habitation, The **1**: 21; **6**: 84

Haiti **1**: 12; **2**: 59; **5**: 19, 22-27; **6**: 7, 9

Hale, John P. **5**: 53

Hale, Sarah Josepha **8**: 70; **9**: 23-24

Hall, Anne **9**: 68

Hall, Fort **4**: 55, 60

Hall, Joseph **9**: 23

Hallam family **9**: 36-37

Hamburg **6**: 30-31

Hamilton, Alexander **1**: 54, 66; **2**: 8-13, 15, 16-19, 23, 27-28, 48, 52, 71; **7**: 9; **9**: 26

Hamlin, Hannibal **5**: 86

Hanby, Benjamin Russell **9**: 53

Hancock, John **1**: 55

handcarts **4**: 70, 72-73; **6**: 19

Handsome Lake **9**: 87

Hargreave, James **10**: 38-39

Harmar, Fort **1**: 49

Harmar, Josiah **2**: 36-37

Harmony **9**: 81

Harpers Ferry **5**: 6, 25, 74, 80-82

Harris, Townsend **5**: 55

Harrison, William Henry **2**: 78, 82; **3**: 75-76; **4**: 6-8, 10; **10**: 68

Hartford Convention **2**: 79-80

Harvard, John **9**: 19

Harvard College (University) **2**: 39; **8**: 11-13, 23, 43, 74; **9**: 13, 15, 19, 30, 64

Hawaii **4**: 65; **10**: 67

Hawthorne, Nathaniel **8**: 87; **9**: 26-27, 29-31

Hayes, Kate **9**: 60

Hayne, Robert **3**: 70

Hays, Mary Ludwig **1**: 41; **7**: 9, 11

heating **7**: 62, 77; **8**: 35-37

Henderson, Thomas **1**: 29

Henry, Joseph **8**: 9, 18-19, 26, 37

Henry, Patrick **1**: 55

Henry, William **5**: 47

Henson, Josiah **5**: 33

Hessians **6**: 62

Hispanic Americans **6**: 82; **9**: 49 (see also Mexican Americans, Spanish Americans, Central Americans)

Hispaniola **1**: 12

history and historians **7**: 9; **9**: 15, 27, 32

Hoban, James **9**: 63-64

Hoe, Richard March **8**: 9

Holmes, Oliver Wendell **2**: 80; **8**: 39; **9**: 26

home production **6**: 56; **7**: 10, 12-13, 62, 65, 67-73, 75-80; **8**: 50, 59-61; **10**: 5, 14, 36, 38, 42, 49

Honduras **5**: 57

Hong Kong **4**: 12; **6**: 29

Hopewell Culture **1**: 50

horses **1**: 16; **2**: 37; **4**: 39; **6**: 77; **8**: 15-16, 24, 51; **10**: 27, 30

Horseshoe Bend **2**: 87; **3**: 77

Hosmer, Harriet **9**: 71

hospitals **8**: 38, 41-43

household managers **7**: 14-18, 59, 62-66; **8**: 46

House of Representatives, U.S. **1**: 59-62, 65; **2**: 47-48, 80; **3**: 58, 63-64, 66, 79; **4**: 8, 17, 23-24; **5**: 41, 53, 59, 69, 74, 79

houses **1**: 15, 22, 49; **3**: 25; **5**: 51, 79; **6**: 15, 41; **7**: 42, 64, 70, 73, 75-77, 81-83; **8**: 27-31, 85 (see also building and construction; architecture and design)

Houston **3**: 79; **6**: 66

Houston, Sam **3**: 39, 77, 79-80; **4**: 13

Howe, Elias **8**: 9

Howe, Julia Ward **5**: 82

Howe, William **1**: 40

Hudson River **1**: 7, 24; **2**: 84; **3**: 7, 15-17, 27-28, 30; **6**: 34, 50; **8**: 17, 19, 33; **9**: 29, 69-70; **10**: 15, 17

Hudson River school **9**: 34, 67, 69-70

Huguenots **1**: 25

Humphreys, Richard **9**: 18

Hunt, Harriot and Sarah **8**: 43

Hunter, Jane **8**: 40

Huron, Lake **1**: 21; **3**: 29

Hussey, Obed **10**: 32

Hussites **6**: 62

Hutin, Francisque **9**: 56

Hutterites **6**: 62

I

ice **3**: 27; **6**: 25; **8**: 56-57, 74

Icelandic Americans **6**: 86

Idaho **2**: 59; **4**: 19, 56, 59, 79, 83; **10**: 63, 66-67

Illinois (people) **3**: 37, 54

Illinois **1**: 49; **2**: 28; **3**: 17-18, 20, 23, 35, 52, 54; **4**: 61, 71, 78; **5**: 29, 34, 59, 75, 77-79, 84, 86; **6**: 70, 87; **7**: 83; **8**: 31; **10**: 11, 13, 22, 63

Imbert, Anthony **6**: 5

immigrants and immigration **1**: 25, 27; **2**: 7, 18, 42; **3**: 13, 17, 21, 27, 36, 75-76; **4**: 35; **6**: 5-87; **8**: 47, 50, 60; **9**: 46, 57, 73, 83-84; **10**: 8-10, 13, 16, 19-20, 49, 60

immigrants, hazards for **6**: 19-23, 25-27, 35

immigrants, transportation of **6**: 5-6, 16-32, 54-55, 59, 63, 67, 75, 79, 87

immigration, costs of **6**: 11, 16, 19, 21-23, 29-31, 41, 55, 63, 80

immigration, reasons for **6**: 6, 8-11, 13-15, 41-46, 59-60, 62-63, 65-67, 74, 78-80, 87

immigration restrictions **6**: 6, 54-55, 63, 83

immigration statistics **6**: 8, 10-16, 40, 42-43, 46, 50, 54-55, 59-61, 64, 67, 70, 75-76, 80, 84-87

impeachment **1**: 62

impressment **2**: 32-33, 72-74, 81

inaugurations, presidential **1**: 27, 65-66, 69; **2**: 48; **3**: 65; **4**: 6, 20; **5**: 83, 87; **8**: 74; **10**: 68

Inca Empire **1**: 12

indentured (bond) servants **6**: 22-23, 63

Independence (city) **3**: 84, 87; **4**: 47, 76

Independence Day **8**: 50, 72

Independence Hall **1**: 37, 56-58, 70, 76; **2**: 7; **8**: 36; **9**: 71

Independence Rock **4**: 51, 53

India **1**: 10, 41; **3**: 6; **4**: 41; **8**: 56

Indian Ocean **1**: 10

Indiana **1**: 49; **2**: 36-37, 77-78; **3**: 17-18, 20, 23, 34, 37, 39, 42-43, 45, 47-48, 52, 54, 81; **4**: 8; **5**: 32, 34, 45, 86; **7**: 40; **8**: 86; **10**: 11, 63

Indian Removal Act **3**: 35-36, 42, 44-45, 48, 65

Indian Wars **1**: 15-16, 22-23, 30 (see also expulsions; Native-American)

Industrial Revolution **6**: 56; **10**: 5, 19, 31, 36-41, 43-44

industry **1**: 30, 51, 53, 83, 86; **2**: 10-12, 18-19; **3**: 26-27, 68; **4**: 37-38, 53; **5**: 51; **6**: 11, 16, 49, 52, 54-58, 60, 71-72; **7**: 60, 64, 67, 70-71, 73, 75, 85-86; **8**: 6-9, 11, 25-26, 61; **9**: 15; **10**: 9, 14, 17, 20-21, 25-26, 28-31, 33, 36-58 (see also mills and factories; manufacturing; business and finance)

Innes, George **9**: 70

Institute for Colored Youth **9**: 18

interchangeable parts **8**: 7, 31-32, 61; **10**: 43-44

inventors and inventions **2**: 18; **7**: 83, 85; **8**: 5-49; **9**: 72; **10**: 28, 31-34, 37-39, 43-44, 57

Iowa **4**: 37, 39, 71, 89; **6**: 70; **10**: 63

Ireland **1**: 25, 81-82; **6**: 7, 38-46; **9**: 83

Irish Americans **2**: 42; **3**: 66; **6**: 7, 9-10, 12-15, 17, 19, 21-22, 26-27, 29, 31, 33, 35, 38-53, 55-56, 59, 61, 65; **9**: 46-47, 73, 82-83; **10**: 16, 20, 24, 61

Irish Sea **6**: 17, 19

iron **6**: 58; **7**: 81-82, 85-86; **8**: 9, 26, 31-34, 36; **10**: 18, 20, 23, 25, 31, 37, 43-44

ironing **7**: 75, 77

Iroquois **9**: 87

Irving, Washington **7**: 40; **9**: 26, 28-29, 40, 60

Italian Americans **6**: 12, 85

Italy **1**: 9-10, 15; **2**: 73; **7**: 31; **9**: 59, 62-63, 71, 83

J

Jackson, Andrew **1**: 77; **2**: 20, 85, 87; **3**: 25, 40, 42, 44, 46, 57, 63-67, 69-77, 80-81; **4**: 13, 15, 17; **5**: 69; **6**: 48; **7**: 17; **9**: 71; **10**: 54, 68

Jackson, Fort **2**: 87

Jackson, Patrick Tracy **10**: 41

Jamaica **5**: 22

Jamestown **1**: 22-23, 85; **2**: 64; **3**: 34, 44; **4**: 80; **5**: 6-7; **10**: 35

Japan **2**: 82; **5**: 54-55

Jay, John **1**: 67, 71; **2**: 32-33, 47; **9**: 27

Jay's Treaty **2**: 32-33, 40-41

Jefferson, Joseph **9**: 37-38

Jefferson, Thomas **1**: 37, 39, 55, 58, 62, 66, 69; **2**: 6, 9-10, 12-13, 16-20, 23, 25, 27-29, 38-39, 43-48, 50-54, 58-59, 62, 64, 67-68, 70-72, 74, 76; **3**: 52, 53, 58; **4**: 40; **5**: 50, 69; **6**:

48, 55; **7**: 9, 16; **8**: 5-6, 22, 44; **9**: 14-15, 19-20, 26, 62-65, 68, 77; **10**: 68

Jennings, Isaiah **8**: 9

Jewett, William S. **4**: 21

Jews **6**: 35, 67, 73-77; **9**: 73, 83

Johnson, Eastman **1**: 41; **9**: 86

Johnson, Madame **8**: 20

Johnson, Richard S. **3**: 75

Johnston, Albert Sidney **4**: 75

Jones, Absalom **9**: 86

Jones, Edward **9**: 18

Juba **9**: 58

judicial branch **1**: 60, 66; **2**: 8

Judiciary Acts **1**: 67; **2**: 49

Judson, Ann Hesseltine **9**: 81

jury trial **1**: 73-74; **5**: 44-46

K

Kanagawa, Treaty of **5**: 55

Kansas **1**: 14; **4**: 28, 47-48, 81; **5**: 38-39, 58-59, 70-72, 74, 81; **8**: 47; **10**: 63

Kansas-Nebraska Act **5**: 6, 38, 58-60, 64, 67-68, 70, 78-79

Kansas River **3**: 84, 87; **4**: 48

Kearny, Stephen **4**: 28-31

Kelley, Abby **7**: 22

Kemble, Fanny **7**: 65

Kensett, John Frederick **9**: 70

Kentucky **1**: 7, 28-30, 45-46; **2**: 29, 45-46, 65-66; **3**: 13, 20-21, 61, 70, 75; **4**: 15; **5**: 42, 84, 86; **6**: 69; **8**: 40-41; **9**: 32, 42, 56, 78; **10**: 11-12, 35, 63

Kentucky Resolution **2**: 45-46

Keokuk **8**: 85

Key, Francis Scott **2**: 84

Kickapoos **3**: 37, 48

kindergarten **9**: 10

King, Charles Bird **2**: 86

King, Fort **3**: 40

King, Martin Luther, Jr. **9**: 32

King, Rufus **3**: 52; **10**: 68

King's College **2**: 12; **9**: 13

Kiowas **3**: 81; **4**: 83-85

Know-Nothing Party **3**: 75; **5**: 41, 64-67, 74, 86; **6**: 48, 53

Knox, Henry **1**: 66

Krug, August **6**: 72

L

labor organizations **7**: 42; **10**: 56-61

Ladies' Christian Association **8**: 76

Lake Champlain, Battle of **2**: 84

Lake of the Woods **4**: 11, 18

Lancaster **3**: 22; **8**: 33

Land Ordinance of 1785 **1**: 47, 49; **9**: 8

land policy and purchases **1**: 29, 47-48, 53; **3**: 17, 55, 73; **9**: 8; **10**: 29

Lane, Fitz Hugh **10**: 47

Lane, Harriet **7**: 17-18

Laramie, Fort **4**: 50, 72, 86

La Salle, Robert Cavelier de **1**: 21

Latin America **3**: 10, 62; **9**: 13

latitude **3**: 8, 60; **4**: 19

Latrobe, Benjamin **6**: 55; **9**: 62, 64-65

Lawrence **5**: 71

Lawrence Scientific School **9**: 15

lawsuits and the law **3**: 45-46; **5**: 18; **7**: 7, 28, 30, 32-42, 52, 55, 65, 85; **8**: 79; **9**: 16 (see also Supreme Court, U.S.; specific cases)

Leavenworth, Fort **4**: 28, 71

LeClerc, Victor **2**: 59

Lecompton (Constitutional Convention) **5**: 71-72

Lee, Ann **9**: 80

Lee, Mary Ann **9**: 56

Lee, Robert E. **5**: 80

legislative branch **1**: 60, 65-66 (see also Congress)

Le Havre **6:** 19, 31
Le Mayeur, Joseph **8:** 45
L'Enfant, Pierre Charles **2:** 48; **9:** 63
Léotard **9:** 45
letters **6:** 13-15, 25, 35, 40-41, 66, 87; **7:** 9, 12-13
Leutze, Emanuel **1:** 40-41; **4:** 5; **9:** 70
Lewis, Meriwether **2:** 67-68; **4:** 40
Lewis and Clark expedition **2:** 1, 64, 67-69; **3:** 87; **4:** 40-41, 46; **8:** 11, 47
Lexington **1:** 35, 40
Liberator, The **3:** 68; **5:** 28-29
Liberty Bell **1:** 76; **3:** 51, 58
Liberty Party **4:** 6, 15
libraries **6:** 54; **9:** 19-21; **10:** 54
Library of Congress **2:** 52; **7:** 29, 46; **9:** 19-20
lighting **8:** 35-37; **10:** 46
Lily, The **8:** 69, 80
Lincoln, Abraham **2:** 6; **3:** 38; **4:** 23-24; **5:** 4, 6, 37, 49, 63, 67-68, 77-79, 83-87; **6:** 71; **7:** 18, 83; **8:** 31, 35, 70, 74; **9:** 39, 72; **10:** 68
Lincoln, Mary Todd **7:** 18
Lincoln University **9:** 18
Lind, Jenny **6:** 36; **9:** 40, 59-60
linens **7:** 67, 75; **8:** 66; **10:** 30
linsey-woolsey **8:** 66
literature **9:** 25-35
Little Turtle **2:** 36-37
Livermore, Mary **7:** 19, 51
Liverpool **6:** 17, 19, 29, 31, 33
Livingston, Henry, Jr. **8:** 72
Livingston, James **2:** 62
locks, canal **3:** 26-27, 29; **8:** 7
log cabin campaign **4:** 7
London (England) **7:** 22, 41; **8:** 32; **9:** 39-41, 43, 67-68
London (Ontario) **2:** 82
London, Treaty of **2:** 32-33
Long, Crawford Williamson **8:** 40-41
Longfellow, Henry Wadsworth **8:** 60; **9:** 26, 34, 75
Long House Religion **9:** 87
Los Angeles **4:** 30-31, 76
Louis XVI, King **2:** 22-26
Louisbourg **2:** 73
Louisiana **2:** 58-69; **3:** 20, 24-25; **5:** 12, 26, 34, 39, 50, 87; **10:** 63
Louisiana Purchase **1:** 21; **2:** 57-64, 66-67, 78; **3:** 60, 77, 82; **4:** 78-79; **5:** 37; **6:** 6, 48; **9:** 82; **10:** 6, 22
Louisville **3:** 20, 29; **10:** 12
L'Ouverture, Toussaint **2:** 59; **5:** 23-24
Lovejoy, E. P. **5:** 29
Lowell **6:** 57; **7:** 42; **8:** 7; **10:** 42, 49, 52-55
Lowell, Francis C. **10:** 41
Loyalists **1:** 35, 37; **9:** 67, 75-76
Ludlow, Noah **9:** 42
Lukens, Rebecca Pennock **7:** 85-86
luminism **9:** 70
Lundy's Lane **2:** 83
Luther, Martin **9:** 47
Lutherans **6:** 62; **9:** 52, 77, 79
Lyell, Charles **8:** 12
Lyndhurst **9:** 65
Lyon, Mary **9:** 16
Lyon, Matthew **2:** 44

M

Macao **4:** 12
Mackenzie, Alexander **4:** 19
Mackinac, Fort **2:** 81
Macon Act **2:** 76
Macready, William **9:** 39
Madison, Dolley **7:** 16-17
Madison, James **1:** 55, 58, 70; **2:** 19, 23, 45-46, 51, 56, 70, 75-76, 78-79; **3:** 52, 53; **7:** 16-17; **9:** 14, 27, 68; **10:** 68
magazines **7:** 65-66, 83; **9:** 21-24
magnetism **8:** 9, 18-19, 26

Maine **1:** 28; **3:** 8, 52, 54, 60; **4:** 11; **5:** 29, 86; **8:** 15; **9:** 34, 65; **10:** 64
Malibran, Maria **9:** 59
Mandans **2:** 68; **4:** 84; **8:** 28
Manhattan Island **10:** 16-17
manifest destiny **4:** 14-15; **5:** 56
Manitoba **6:** 60
Mann, Horace **9:** 9-10
Mansfield, Arabella Babb **7:** 28
manufacturing **1:** 51; **2:** 72; **3:** 68; **4:** 68; **6:** 16; **10:** 18, 23, 32, 39-44 (see also mills and factories; industry)
Marbury v. Madison **2:** 53
Marietta **1:** 49; **2:** 65
Maroons **5:** 22-23
Marquette, Jacques **1:** 19
marriage **3:** 41; **4:** 70, 74-75; **6:** 23; **7:** 18, 23, 30, 32, 35-40, 42, 58, 64; **8:** 87
Marseilles **4:** 38
Marseilles **4:** 38
Marshall, James **4:** 64
Marshall, John **2:** 49, 53; **3:** 46, 50-51, 57, 74
Martin v. Hunter's Lessee **3:** 51
Martineau, Harriet **10:** 54
Maryland **1:** 44, 82, 84; **2:** 48, 83-84; **3:** 17, 23, 50, 57, 67, 74; **4:** 39; **5:** 13, 80, 86; **6:** 33, 47, 62, 69; **8:** 19, 37; **9:** 14, 52, 75; **10:** 19, 64
Masonic Order **3:** 75
Massachusetts **1:** 24, 35-36, 54-55, 63-64, 71, 82, 84-85; **2:** 9, 38-39, 79; **3:** 17-18, 54, 64, 70; **5:** 31, 45-46, 67; **6:** 28, 33, 57; **7:** 11, 20, 25, 28, 30, 34, 50, 54-55; **8:** 7, 17, 22-23, 33, 46, 74, 84, 87; **9:** 6-7, 9-10, 13, 16, 19-20, 31, 33-35, 52, 65, 74-75; **10:** 12-13, 41-42, 46-47, 49, 52-55, 60-61, 64
Massachusetts Institute of Technology **8:** 8-9; **9:** 16
massacres **1:** 35; **4:** 75, 86-87; **5:** 24-25, 27-28 (see also specific events)
Matamoros **4:** 21, 25
mathematics **8:** 7, 22-23
Maumee River **2:** 37
Maximilian, Emperor **3:** 10
Mayflower **1:** 24, 26
Maywood, Augusta **9:** 56
McClintock, Mary **7:** 44, 56
McCormick, Cyrus **8:** 9; **10:** 31-32
McCulloch v. Maryland **3:** 50, 57
McDowell, Ephraim **8:** 40-41
McHenry, Fort **2:** 84
medicine and health care **3:** 47; **4:** 8; **5:** 33; **6:** 28, 45-46; **7:** 10, 58, 85; **8:** 9, 11, 38-49, 75; **9:** 16, 24, 81
Mediterranean Sea **1:** 9; **2:** 54-55; **8:** 14
Meigs, Fort **2:** 82
Melville, Herman **9:** 30
Memphis **3:** 25; **5:** 61
Mendelssohn, Moses **9:** 84
Mennonites **1:** 26; **6:** 62
mental health care **7:** 42; **8:** 44-45, 75
Merrimack River **8:** 33; **10:** 42, 52
Merry, Anne Brunton **9:** 37
metals and metalworking **6:** 58; **7:** 81-82, 85-86; **8:** 7, 9, 25-26, 31-34, 36, 57, 59-60; **10:** 18, 20, 23, 25, 31-32, 37, 43-44 (see also gold; silver)
Methodists **5:** 29, 51; **9:** 15, 47, 77-79, 85-86
Mexican Americans **4:** 69; **6:** 12; **9:** 82-83
Mexican-American War **1:** 17; **2:** 57; **3:** 9, 44, 76, 86; **4:** 5, 16, 20-34, 37, 43, 62, 64, 71, 77-78, 81; **5:** 36-37, 39, 41, 52-53, 57; **9:** 82; **10:** 7
Mexican Revolution **1:** 8; **3:** 9, 77, 82; **4:** 78
Mexico **1:** 8, 12, 15-17, 21; **2:** 57, 63; **3:** 9, 10, 44, 48, 68, 76-78, 84, 86; **4:** 5, 13, 15-16, 18, 20-34, 37, 45, 62, 65, 78; **5:** 32, 35, 41, 47, 57; **10:** 6-7
Mexico, Gulf of **1:** 7, 21; **2:** 34, 59, 63; **3:** 15, 21, 24-25; **4:** 26, 81; **5:** 14; **6:** 50

Mexico City **3:** 82; **4:** 25-27, 32-33
Miamis **3:** 36-37; **3:** 37
Michigames **3:** 37
Michigan **1:** 49; **3:** 17-18, 29, 54; **4:** 78; **5:** 39, 46, 68, 87; **10:** 64
Michigan, Lake **1:** 21; **3:** 57
Midnight Judges **2:** 49
Midwest **1:** 21; **3:** 17, 28, 68; **4:** 35, 38; **6:** 6, 70-72, 87; **10:** 26
Military Road **3:** 25
militias, state **1:** 55, 68-69, 72; **2:** 14, 46, 81; **5:** 17
Miller, Elizabeth Smith **8:** 69
Miller, Frederick **6:** 72
Miller, William **9:** 80
Mills, Robert **9:** 64-65
mills and factories **1:** 52-53; **6:** 9, 11, 56-58, 72; **7:** 63, 81, 84, 87; **8:** 7, 24-26, 28, 30-31, 34, 50, 61, 75; **10:** 5, 14, 23, 25, 28-30, 36, 38-44, 49-58
Milwaukee **6:** 70, 72
Mims, Fort **2:** 87
Miner, Myrtilla **9:** 18
miners and mining **3:** 84; **4:** 66-68, 86; **6:** 53, 57-58, 66, 78, 81-82
Minnesota **3:** 6; **4:** 11, 37, 39, 79; **10:** 1, 64
minstrel shows **9:** 41-42, 52-53
missions and missionaries **1:** 18-19, 21, 86-87; **3:** 9-10, 86; **4:** 69; **6:** 78, 85; **9:** 73, 81
Mississippi **2:** 86; **3:** 9, 20, 24-25, 27, 44-45, 48, 52, 54, 55, 68-69; **5:** 12, 16, 34, 57, 87; **7:** 36; **10:** 62, 64
Mississippi River **1:** 16, 21, 33, 41, 45, 51, 87; **2:** 34-36, 58-59, 63-64, 67; **3:** 9, 17, 20, 22, 23, 25, 30-31, 33-39, 44-45, 47-48, 66, 82, 86; **4:** 35-37, 40, 47, 56, 71, 79-82, 84; **5:** 14, 22-23, 51; **6:** 6, 15, 34, 50, 52, 62, 64, 68-70; **8:** 15, 17-18; **9:** 33, 42, 45; **10:** 5-6, 15, 21-22, 25
Missouri **2:** 68; **3:** 18, 20, 23, 52, 54, 58-61, 82, 84; **4:** 40-43, 47-48, 70; **5:** 61-62, 70-72, 75; **6:** 34, 66, 70-71; **10:** 11, 22, 64
Missouri Compromise of 1820 **1:** 77; **3:** 53-54, 58-61; **5:** 29, 37-39, 58, 75, 79
Missouri Fur Company **2:** 69
Missouri River **1:** 21; **2:** 58, 62, 68; **3:** 31, 84, 87; **4:** 40, 42, 44, 46, 49, 71-72, 84; **8:** 10; **10:** 22, 26
Mitchell, Maria **7:** 42; **8:** 23
Mobile **1:** 41; **2:** 87; **3:** 25
Mohawk River **1:** 28, 45, 78; **3:** 15-19, 26, 28
Mohawks **1:** 78
Mohawk Trail **1:** 7, 45; **2:** 65; **3:** 12, 14, 15-19, 21, 26, 33
Molino del Rey **4:** 33
money **1:** 60; **2:** 7, 16-17; **3:** 57, 72; **4:** 17; **7:** 60, 65-67 (see also banks; credit; financial; debts and debtors)
Monroe, James **1:** 55; **2:** 59, 62, 75; **3:** 52-53, 62, 64; **9:** 68; **10:** 68
Monroe Doctrine **3:** 53, 62
Montana **2:** 59; **3:** 31; **4:** 19, 46, 59, 79, 83; **10:** 64, 66-67
Monterey **4:** 30
Monterrey **4:** 25-26
Monticello **2:** 50, 70; **8:** 6, 22; **9:** 63, 65
Montreal **2:** 82, 84; **3:** 19
Moore, Charles Herbert **10:** 16
Moore, Clement Clarke **8:** 72
Moran, Thomas **2:** 59, 64; **4:** 60, 74
Moravians **6:** 61-62
Mormons **4:** 5, 44, 55, 60, 62, 70-75, 77, 87; **9:** 80
Mormon Trail **4:** 44, 72-73
Morocco **2:** 54
Morris, George **9:** 23
Morse, Samuel F. B. **3:** 49; **8:** 9, 19; **9:** 69, 72
Morton, William Thomas Green **8:** 9, 41
Mott, James **7:** 44-46, 50
Mott, Jordan Lawrence **8:** 9s

Mott, Lucretia Coffin **4:** 17; **7:** 21-23, 41, 43-47, 50-51, 53, 55; **8:** 62
Mount, William Sydney **9:** 70
Mountain Meadows **4:** 75
Mount Holyoke Female Seminary (College) **9:** 16-17
Mount Vernon **1:** 68-69; **5:** 5; **8:** 29
Mowatt, Anna **9:** 40
museums **8:** 11, 13, 19; **9:** 20
music and musical instruments **6:** 72; **9:** 11, 25, 46-60
Muslims **1:** 9

N

Nantucket **7:** 50; **8:** 23
Napoleonic Wars **2:** 24, 26, 30, 34, 55-59, 62, 84-85; **3:** 5, 6, 9, 10; **6:** 5, 30, 54, 63-64, 69, 86; **10:** 19, 35, 46
Nashville **1:** 45; **5:** 43; **3:** 20, 66
Nassau, Fort **1:** 24
Nast, Thomas **6:** 83; **8:** 71
Natchez **3:** 20-21, 25
National Academy of Design **9:** 68
National Republican Party **2:** 20; **3:** 64, 71, 75 (see also Whigs)
National Road (Pike) **3:** 5, 14, 21, 23
Native American Party **3:** 75; **5:** 65-67
Native Americans **1:** 7-8, 12-16, 18-19, 22-24, 26, 29, 45-47, 50, 58, 71, 78, 81, 86-87; **2:** 18, 33, 35-37, 58, 62, 64, 66-69, 77-79, 81-83, 86-87; **3:** 8, 12, 14, 17, 24, 34-48, 65, 79-81, 83, 85-86; **4:** 18, 44, 46-49, 55, 58-59, 68-69, 71, 77, 80-87; **5:** 9, 47, 63, 66; **6:** 47, 82; **7:** 13, 61, 68, 72; **8:** 27, 39-40, 46-47, 56, 62, 67; **9:** 12-13, 27, 34, 40, 54-55, 70, 73, 87; **10:** 10-11, 29, 45, 65 (see also specific peoples; expulsions, Native-American)
natural increase **1:** 27; **3:** 12; **10:** 9-10
Naturalization Act **2:** 18, 42-43
nature and naturalists **8:** 10-14; **9:** 31-32, 34, 69-70, 85, 87
Nauvoo **4:** 71
Navajos **4:** 85
naval forces **1:** 86; **2:** 8, 30, 32, 40-41, 51-52, 72-74, 81, 84; **4:** 21, 29, 32; **5:** 11; **8:** 14 (see also armed forces, U.S.; sailors)
Navidad **1:** 16
navigation **8:** 22-23
Nebraska **3:** 75; **4:** 51, 71, 83; **5:** 58-59; **10:** 65
Necessity, Fort **1:** 68
Negro Fort **3:** 41
Nelson, Horatio **2:** 73
Netherlands **1:** 15, 24, 53, 81-82, 84-85; **2:** 26, 39; **3:** 64; **5:** 6; **6:** 75, 86; **9:** 73 (see also Dutch Americans)
neutrality **2:** 28-30, 40, 72; **10:** 47
Nevada **4:** 34, 43, 60, 62, 74; **9:** 34; **10:** 65
New Amsterdam **1:** 24; **6:** 75; **9:** 28
Newark **10:** 17
New Bedford **10:** 46
New Braunfels **6:** 66
New Brunswick **3:** 8; **4:** 11
New Echota **3:** 46
Newell, Harriet **9:** 81
New England **1:** 24, 31, 45, 52-53, 84; **2:** 32, 72, 74-75, 79; **3:** 17, 56-18, 68; **5:** 35, 67; **6:** 48; **7:** 9, 31; **8:** 26, 70, 78; **9:** 7, 29, 31-32, 38, 57, 63, 76-77, 83; **10:** 19, 30, 41-42, 45-46, 49-51, 61
New England Anti-Slavery Society **5:** 30, 70; **7:** 21, 24
Newfoundland **1:** 14-15, 19; **10:** 45
New France **1:** 21
New Hampshire **1:** 26, 64, 82, 85; **5:** 53; **8:** 33, 85; **10:** 58, 65
New Harmony **7:** 40; **8:** 86
New Jersey **1:** 40-41, 64, 82, 84; **2:** 76; **3:** 17; **6:** 70; **7:** 5, 7, 11; **8:** 20, 25; **9:** 75; **10:** 12, 17, 58, 65

New Jersey, College of **9:** 13
New Mexico **3:** 82-85; **4:** 28, 31, 34, 50, 76-77, 84-85; **5:** 43, 57, 59; **7:** 74; **10:** 65 (see also Nuevo Mexico)
New Netherlands **1:** 24, 85
New Orleans **1:** 41, 51; **2:** 34-35, 58-59, 62, 85; **3:** 6, 17, 21, 25, 30, 40, 84; **5:** 12, 14, 24, 26, 50; **6:** 27, 34, 50-51, 62, 64, 69; **8:** 39; **9:** 38, 49, 54, 60; **10:** 14, 21-22, 26
New Orleans, Battle of **3:** 40, 66
Newport **6:** 73, 75, 77; **9:** 19
New Salem **5:** 84
newspapers and journalists **7:** 19, 31, 55, 57; **9:** 21-23, 33-34; **10:** 59 (see also press, freedom of)
New Sweden **6:** 86
New York Anti-Slavery Society **5:** 18
New York City **1:** 24, 26, 40, 52, 63, 65-67, 69, 83; **2:** 71, 84; **3:** 17, 19, 27, 30; **4:** 38; **5:** 18, 35, 62; **6:** 5, 9, 23, 31, 33-34, 36-37, 50, 52-53, 69-70, 75, 86; **7:** 11, 15, 28; **8:** 8, 19-21, 30, 32, 39, 42-43, 50, 57, 64, 72-74, 76; **9:** 23-24, 28, 36-43, 45, 48, 52, 56, 59-60, 70, 72, 83; **10:** 9, 14-19, 22-23, 26, 50, 56, 58-59
New York State **1:** 31, 40, 45, 63-64, 82, 84-85; **2:** 5-6, 38, 70-71; **3:** 7, 14-19, 26-30, 33, 68, 76; **4:** 15, 17, 24, 70; **5:** 17, 25, 34, 40, 47, 67; **6:** 5, 33-34, 47, 52, 62, 75; **7:** 11, 26, 28, 31, 36, 41-47, 50, 55-56; **8:** 34, 43-44, 51, 68, 78-80, 82-84, 87; **9:** 28, 75, 80-81; **10:** 6, 9, 12-17, 27, 65
New York Tribune **4:** 23; **7:** 31; **8:** 86; **9:** 23
Nicaragua **5:** 56-57
Nogales, Treaty of **2:** 36
Non-Intercourse Act **2:** 74, 76
Norse **1:** 14
North, Levi **9:** 45
North Africa **2:** 54-55
North and Northerners **2:** 6; **3:** 60, 68, 81; **4:** 13, 20, 22, 37-39, 78; **5:** 5, 17-21, 25, 28, 30, 32-35, 37-38, 40, 43-51, 56, 58-59, 61, 64, 67-70, 73-74, 78-79, 82-83; **6:** 11, 33, 58; **7:** 19-20, 52, 55, 64, 68; **8:** 56, 66, 73; **9:** 15, 18, 77-78, 86; **10:** 14, 17, 20, 30, 43
North Carolina **1:** 64, 82, 85; **3:** 20, 25; **4:** 17; **5:** 31, 87; **6:** 62; **9:** 14, 49; **10:** 65
North Carolina, University of **4:** 17; **9:** 14
North Dakota **2:** 68; **4:** 83; **10:** 26, 65
North Sea **6:** 19
Northwest Ordinance **1:** 49-50, 71; **3:** 54; **5:** 69; **9:** 8
Northwest Territory **1:** 49-50, 71; **2:** 18, 33, 66; **3:** 54, 78-79
Norwegian Americans **6:** 12, 14-15, 19, 25, 35, 86-87; **9:** 79
Nott, Eliphalet **8:** 9
Nova Scotia **1:** 21; **2:** 73; **6:** 84; **9:** 34
novels and novelists **9:** 27-28, 30, 32
Noyes, John Humphrey **8:** 87
Nueces River **4:** 21, 34
Nuevo León **4:** 25
Nuevo Mexico **1:** 17; **2:** 69; **3:** 9, 82-85, 87
nullification **3:** 58, 67-71
nurses **3:** 86; **6:** 46; **7:** 11, 85; **8:** 41-42, 44-45
nutrition **8:** 49, 55
Nuttall, Thomas **8:** 11

O

Oberlin Collegiate Institute (College) **7:** 27, 38; **9:** 17-18
obstetricians **8:** 46-47
Oceanian Americans **6:** 12
Ohio **1:** 6, 49-50, 53; **2:** 8, 37, 65-66; **3:** 12, 17-18, 23, 30, 37, 54; **4:** 8, 70; **5:** 34; **6:** 34, 68-69; **7:** 27-28, 54; **8:** 57; **9:** 16, 32, 84; **10:** 11, 13, 24, 36, 65
Ohio River **1:** 45, 49; **2:** 35, 37, 66; **3:** 17, 20, 22-23, 27-29, 31; **6:** 52; **9:** 42; **10:** 12, 24
oils **8:** 35-36; **10:** 45-46
Ojibwas **3:** 34, 37; **9:** 34
Oklahoma **3:** 34, 39, 42-43, 47, 81; **4:** 81, 83; **10:** 67
Old American Company **9:** 37, 56
Old Northwest **1:** 49, 86; **2:** 18, 36-37, 77, 81, 83, 86; **3:** 26, 37, 44, 48, 56, 68; **4:** 8, 81; **6:** 13, 64; **10:** 13
Old Southwest **2:** 86-87; **3:** 24-25, 35, 39, 44, 56, 58, 65
Omaha **3:** 75; **4:** 71-72
Omahas **4:** 71, 83
Omnibus Bill **5:** 41-43
Oñate, Don Juan de **1:** 17
Oneida Community **8:** 68-69, 87
Ontario, Lake **3:** 15; **10:** 6
opera **9:** 25, 59-60
Opium Wars **4:** 12; **5:** 54; **6:** 79-80
Oregon **1:** 16; **2:** 68-69; **3:** 8, 9, 11, 87; **4:** 11, 15-16, 18-19, 34, 37, 39, 41-48, 51, 54-59, 79, 83, 87; **5:** 36-37; **10:** 7, 66
Oregon Trail **1:** 7; **4:** 5, 41-42, 44-57, 60, 63, 72; **5:** 62
Oregon Treaty **4:** 11, 16, 18-19, 79, 81; **5:** 36
Orleans, Territory of **2:** 66
Osceola **3:** 40, 42-43
Otis, Elisha **8:** 32
Overland Trail **4:** 44
Owen, Robert Dale **7:** 40; **8:** 85-86

P

Pacific coast **1:** 16, 87; **2:** 68; **3:** 11; **4:** 5, 15, 18-19, 36, 38, 40-43, 45-46, 51, 64, 66, 81-82, 84; **6:** 29, 35, 48, 50, 80, 87; **8:** 15, 18, 20; **9:** 42, 61; **10:** 5, 7
Pacific Northwest **1:** 7, 52; **2:** 34; **3:** 86-87; **4:** 5, 11, 15, 18-19, 44, 57-59, 83; **7:** 68
Pacific Ocean **1:** 87; **3:** 87; **4:** 29, 45-46, 65-66; **6:** 5, 29, 78-80; **9:** 30; **10:** 19, 46
packets **6:** 30-32 (see also sailing ships; steamships)
Paine, Thomas **2:** 24-25; **7:** 58; **9:** 26
painters and painting **6:** 85; **9:** 61, 66-70
Paiutes **7:** 82
Pakenham, Edward **2:** 85
Palladio, Andrea **9:** 62
Palmer, Timothy **8:** 33
Palo Alto **4:** 22, 25
Palos **1:** 10
Panama **4:** 63, 65-66
Panic of 1819 **3:** 50, 52, 55-57, 72
Panic of 1837 **3:** 29, 33, 72-73, 75-76; **6:** 13; **10:** 60
paper **6:** 72; **8:** 76; **9:** 22-23, 72
Paris **1:** 43-44; **2:** 22
Parkman, Francis **4:** 45; **9:** 32
parties, political **2:** 7, 19, 21; **3:** 71
Parton, Sara Willis Payson **7:** 81
Passenger Acts **6:** 54
Pastorius, Franz Daniel **6:** 62
Paterson **10:** 58
Pawnees **4:** 83
Pawtucket **6:** 56; **10:** 40-42, 58
Payne, John Howard **9:** 40
Peabody, Elizabeth **9:** 10
Peale, Charles Willson, and family **2:** 46; **7:** 87; **8:** 11, 13; **9:** 20, 68-69
peddlers **6:** 75, 77; **8:** 60-61; **9:** 84
Peirce, Benjamin **8:** 23
Penn, William **1:** 24, 79, 84
Pennsylvania **1:** 24-26, 28, 31-33, 40, 42, 45, 58, 63-64, 68, 70-71, 76-77, 82, 84-85; **2:** 5-6, 14; **3:** 14, 17, 21, 33, 68; **4:** 24; **5:** 29, 34, 73; **6:** 33-34, 47, 62, 68, 75, 77; **8:** 6, 20, 33, 36, 42, 83-84; **9:** 20, 42, 67, 81, 85; **10:** 12-13, 18, 24-25, 38, 66
Pennsylvania, College (University) of **8:** 6, 43-44; **9:** 7, 13
Pennsylvania Abolition Society **5:** 29
Pennsylvania Academy of Fine Arts **9:** 20, 68
Pennsylvania Avenue **5:** 52; **9:** 62
Pennsylvania Land Company **1:** 30
Pennsylvania Road **1:** 45; **3:** 14, 21-22; **10:** 24
Pensacola **1:** 17, 42; **3:** 42
Peorias **3:** 37
performing arts **9:** 36-60
Perry, Matthew Calbraith **2:** 81; **5:** 54-55
Perry, Oliver Hazard **2:** 79, 81; **5:** 55
personal liberty laws **5:** 45-46
Peru **1:** 12; **3:** 9
Philadelphia **1:** 24, 37, 40, 45, 56-59, 64, 70, 76, 79, 82; **2:** 16-17, 19, 48, 84; **3:** 22, 28, 29, 51; **6:** 7, 33-34, 47, 49, 62, 68-70, 74-75; **7:** 9, 12-13, 15, 21, 26, 45; **8:** 5-7, 20, 30, 33, 36, 39, 42, 44, 74, 83; **9:** 8, 18-20, 36-3, 39, 43, 52, 56, 71, 81, 85-86; **10:** 11, 14, 18-19, 38, 40, 56, 58
Philadelphia, College of **9:** 13
Philadelphia College of Surgeons **4:** 8
Philadelphia Female Anti-Slavery Society **7:** 21, 50
Philharmonic Society of New York **9:** 49
Phillips, Wendell **5:** 17; **7:** 55, 58
philosophy **9:** 15, 31-32
photography **9:** 72
physicians **3:** 86; **6:** 46, 71; **7:** 38; **8:** 13, 38-47
physics **8:** 7, 22
Pierce, Franklin **5:** 52-54, 56-59, 68; **10:** 68
Pike, Zebulon **2:** 64, 69
Pilgrims **1:** 24, 26, 84; **8:** 70
Pinckney, Charles Cotesworth **2:** 47, 70, 75; **10:** 68
Pinckney, Thomas **2:** 34-35, 38, 47
Pinckney's Treaty **2:** 34-36; **3:** 9
Pitcher, Molly **1:** 41; **7:** 9, 11
Pitt, Fort **1:** 32; **10:** 24
Pittman, John W. **5:** 15
Pittsburgh **1:** 32-33, 45, 68; **3:** 22, 28, 29, 30; **6:** 52, 66; **8:** 34; **9:** 42, 51; **10:** 14, 21, 24-25
Placide, Alexander **9:** 55-56
plains and prairies **1:** 16; **3:** 82, 84, 86-87; **4:** 5, 48-50, 52, 60, 70, 83-86; **6:** 6; **10:** 32
planters and plantations **1:** 22, 31, 48, 53, 69; **3:** 12, 24, 55-56, 68; **4:** 9, 16-17, 36; **5:** 9, 12-14, 17, 26, 28, 50-51; **7:** 25, 65, 78; **8:** 29, 52, 60, 64; **10:** 29 (see also farms and farmers; specific crops)
Platte River **3:** 75, 87; **4:** 48-50, 72
Plattsburgh **2:** 8
playwrights **7:** 9; **9:** 27, 36-37, 40-41
Plymouth **1:** 24
Pocahontas **1:** 23; **9:** 40
Poe, Edgar Allan **9:** 27, 33
poets and poetry **1:** 36; **2:** 84; **8:** 70; **9:** 23, 27, 31, 33-35, 75
Polish Americans **6:** 85
Polk, James K. **4:** 15-17, 19-21, 24-25, 29, 31, 43, 65; **6:** 48; **7:** 17; **10:** 68
Polk, Sarah **7:** 18
Ponce de León, Juan **1:** 15
Pony Express **4:** 48; **5:** 60, 61-63; **8:** 18
population **1:** 27-28, 79-83, 86; **3:** 13, 21, 26, 49, 58; **4:** 36-37, 69, 78; **5:** 76; **6:** 16, 42, 67, 79; **7:** 87; **8:** 50, 60; **9:** 5, 24; **10:** 5-6, 8-14, 16-20, 22-26, 29, 37, 62-67
portages **1:** 20; **3:** 10, 19
Port-au-Prince **5:** 24
Portland (ME) **9:** 34
Portland (OR) **4:** 58
Portolá, Gaspar de **1:** 18
Port Royal **1:** 21; **6:** 84
Portugal **1:** 10, 12, 15; **2:** 73, 80; **5:** 7; **6:** 75, 77; **9:** 48; **10:** 45
Portuguese Americans **6:** 85; **9:** 73, 84
potato famine **6:** 14, 29, 44-46, 65
Potawatomis **3:** 35
Potomac River **2:** 48; **5:** 52; **8:** 34
Pottawatomie Creek **5:** 71-72
Poulton, George R. **9:** 53
power, for work **8:** 7, 24-26; **10:** 33
Power, Tyrone **9:** 39
Powers, Hiram **9:** 71
Powhatans **1:** 23; **9:** 40
Presbyterians **5:** 18; **7:** 18; **9:** 15, 77, 79
Presidency, U.S. **1:** 60-62, 65-67; **2:** 43, 47-48, 70; **3:** 40, 52-53, 66; **10:** 68 (see also specific presidents)
President's House: See White House
press, freedom of the **1:** 72; **2:** 44
Price, Stephen **9:** 38
Priestley, Joseph **8:** 6
Prigg v. Pennsylvania **5:** 46
Princeton University **2:** 76; **9:** 13
printing **1:** 59; **7:** 87; **8:** 9, 76; **9:** 21-24, 52; **10:** 56
prisons and prisoners **5:** 14; **6:** 22; **7:** 42; **8:** 44, 75, 82-84
private property **1:** 73
probable cause **1:** 73
Prophetstown **2:** 77-78
proslavery activities **3:** 74; **4:** 15, 37-38, 69; **5:** 37-38, 43, 50-52, 56-59, 61, 67, 70-72, 78; **7:** 23 (see also slaves and slavery)
Prosser, Gabriel **5:** 25-27
Protestants **1:** 25; **2:** 42; **3:** 86; **5:** 67; **6:** 7, 34, 38-41, 47-48, 61-62, 78; **9:** 14-15, 47, 58, 73, 74-83, 85, 87 (see also specific groups)
Providence **7:** 30; **10:** 41
Prussia **2:** 24; **3:** 64
public speaking, by women **7:** 6, 21, 24-28; **9:** 11, 81
publishing **6:** 71; **7:** 65-66, 83, 86-87; **9:** 21-24
Pueblos **1:** 16
punishment, cruel and unusual **1:** 75 (see also prisons and prisoners)
Puritans **1:** 24; **6:** 48; **9:** 29, 47, 57, 77

Q

Quakers **1:** 24, 26; **2:** 5-6; **5:** 10, 29; **6:** 62; **7:** 19, 21, 26, 44, 50, 58; **9:** 18, 67, 77
quartering of soldiers **1:** 35, 72
Quebec **1:** 19, 21; **6:** 33
Queens College **9:** 13
Queenston **2:** 81
Quidor, John **9:** 61
Quitman, John **5:** 57

R

rafts **3:** 16, 56; **4:** 49; **6:** 47
railroads **1:** 83; **3:** 12, 18, 21-23, 28-29, 32-33; **4:** 35-36, 56; **5:** 57-58, 60, 62; **6:** 16, 49, 52, 58, 82-83; **8:** 6-7, 9, 17, 21, 26, 56-57, 63; **9:** 42, 44-45; **10:** 14, 16, 18, 20, 23, 26, 39, 42-43
Randolph, Edmund **1:** 66
Rankin, Jean and John **5:** 33
Rappites **8:** 85-86; **9:** 80-81
reading **9:** 6-9, 12, 21-24
Reed, Esther DeBerdt **7:** 10
reform dress **8:** 68-69, 81
Reformed Church **6:** 62
reformers, social and political **6:** 64, 71; **7:** 6, 19, 42, 44, 58; **8:** 44-45, 75-87; **9:** 30-31; **10:** 55, 59, 61 (see also specific movements)
Reichardt, Ferdinand **4:** 37
Reign of Terror **2:** 25-27, 29, 41; **7:** 32
religion **1:** 24-25, 71-72, 85; **5:** 19, 51; **7:** 26-28; **8:** 85; **9:** 6-10, 14-16, 31, 47-48, 53-55, 57-58, 73-87 (see also missions and missionaries; specific groups)
religion, African-American **9:** 18, 81, 85-86
religion, freedom of **1:** 71-72, 85; **6:** 41, 61-62, 64, 73-74, 87; **7:** 23; **9:** 10, 74, 76-77
religion, women in **7:** 26-28, 50, 85
religious revivals **7:** 26; **8:** 76; **9:** 15, 74, 77-79
Remington, Frederic **3:** 87; **4:** 54; **5:** 63
Rensselaer Polytechnic Institute **9:** 15

Republicans (antislavery) **2:** 20; **5:** 6, 37, 53, 64, 68-69, 73, 76-79, 82, 85-86; **6:** 71; **7:** 6, 19; **10:** 68
Republicans (French) **2:** 22-27, 40-41
Republicans (Jeffersonian) **2:** 9, 15-16, 19-20, 29, 38-39, 41, 43-48, 50-52, 70, 75-76, 79; **3:** 63-64, 69; **8:** 78-79; **9:** 27; **10:** 68
Resaca de la Palma **4:** 22
Rhode Island **1:** 57, 64, 71, 82, 85; **2:** 79; **6:** 56, 73, 75, 77; **7:** 30; **9:** 19, 84; **10:** 40-42, 52, 57, 66
Rice, Dan **9:** 45
Richmond **5:** 26, 47; **9:** 63-64
Ricketts, John Bill **9:** 43, 45
Rio Grande **1:** 17; **2:** 58; **4:** 21-22, 25-26, 28, 34
roads and trails **1:** 45, 48, 51, 82; **3:** 5, 12-27; **4:** 35, 39; **6:** 16, 49, 52; **8:** 15-16; **9:** 44; **10:** 23 (see also specific roads)
Robespierre, Maximilien **2:** 25
Rochambeau, Jean Baptiste de **1:** 42
Rochester **6:** 52; **7:** 45, 51; **10:** 24
Rockford Female Seminary (College) **9:** 17
Rocky Mountain Fur Company **3:** 87
Rocky Mountains **1:** 21; **2:** 58, 63, 67-69; **3:** 8, 15, 17, 86-87; **4:** 5, 18, 41, 45, 48-51, 54, 85; **5:** 38; **6:** 6; **10:** 6
Roebling, John **8:** 34
Rogers, Randolph **9:** 71
Romanticism **9:** 31, 69
Rome (Italy) **9:** 62-63
Rome (NY) **3:** 17
Rose, Ernestine **7:** 36
Ross, Betsy **7:** 8
Ross, Fort **3:** 11
Ross, John **3:** 46
Rotterdam **6:** 19
Ruggles, David **5:** 33
Rush, Benjamin **8:** 38, 43-45, 77-78; **9:** 14
Rush, William **9:** 71
Rush-Bagot Agreement **3:** 8
Russell, Alfred **2:** 67
Russia **1:** 15, 81, 87; **3:** 11, 64; **4:** 18; **5:** 74; **6:** 64
Russian Americans **6:** 85
Russwurm, John **9:** 18
Rutgers University **9:** 13

S

Sacagawea **2:** 67-68
Sacramento **4:** 60, 62, 64; **5:** 63; **8:** 20
Sacramento River **4:** 31
sailors **2:** 72-74, 81; **6:** 23, 78; **9:** 30, 47; **10:** 19, 46-47 (see also naval forces)
St. Augustine **1:** 17; **2:** 78; **5:** 25
St. Clair, Arthur **2:** 37
St. George, Fort **1:** 42
St. Joseph **5:** 62
St. Lawrence River and Gulf **1:** 15, 19-21
St. Louis **2:** 68-69; **3:** 23; **4:** 40-41, 47; **5:** 61-62; **6:** 34, 52, 69-70; **10:** 14, 22-23
St. Marks **3:** 42
St. Mary's Falls **3:** 29
St. Nicholas **8:** 71
St. Paul **10:** 1
Salem **2:** 9; **5:** 31; **7:** 20; **9:** 20
Salem Anti-Slavery Society **5:** 31
Saltillo **4:** 26, 31
Salt Lake City (Valley) **4:** 43, 55, 60, 71, 73, 75; **5:** 63
Sampson, Deborah **7:** 11
San Antonio **3:** 77-79; **10:** 7
San Diego **1:** 16, 18; **4:** 29-30, 71, 76; **10:** 7
San Francisco **1:** 87; **4:** 30, 65-66, 68; **5:** 61-62; **6:** 29, 80-82; **9:** 60, 73; **10:** 14, 61
San Jacinto **3:** 78-79
San Lorenzo, Treaty of **2:** 34-35
San Pascual **4:** 29
San Salvador **1:** 12
Santa Anna, Antonio López de **3:** 79, 81; **4:** 26-27, 32
Santa Barbara **4:** 30
Santa Claus **8:** 71
Santa Fe (Trail) **1:** 17; **3:** 82-85; **4:** 28-29, 31, 47-48, 71, 76; **7:** 74
Santo Domingo **5:** 24; **9:** 38, 55
Saratoga **1:** 40; **8:** 78
Sauk **3:** 37-38, 48
Savannah **3:** 31; **6:** 31-32
Savannah **6:** 33, 75; **10:** 14
Saxton, Joseph **8:** 9
Scandinavian Americans **6:** 84, 86-87; **9:** 79
Schenectady **3:** 19; **6:** 52
schools **1:** 47; **7:** 13, 60, 63, 66; **8:** 54; **9:** 5-12, 57, 83
Schurz, Carl **6:** 71
Schurz, Margarethe **9:** 10
Schussele, Christian **8:** 9; **9:** 26
Schuylkill River **6:** 33; **8:** 33
science and technology **8:** 5-49; **9:** 15, 20; **10:** 37-39
Scotch-Irish **1:** 25; **6:** 34, 39-40, 47-48
Scotland **1:** 25, 81-82; **6:** 7; **9:** 25
Scott, Winfield **4:** 26, 32-34; **5:** 52-53; **10:** 68
Scottish Americans **6:** 7, 17, 54, 57; **9:** 46-47
Scott's Bluff **4:** 51
Scull, John **9:** 23
sculptors **6:** 85; **9:** 66, 71
search and seizure **1:** 73
Seattle, Chief **4:** 83; **8:** 14
secession **1:** 77; **2:** 79; **3:** 53, 58, 67-70, 80; **4:** 10; **5:** 5-6, 36, 41, 43, 47, 48, 52, 56, 58-59, 73-74, 76, 82-83, 87
Secretary of State, U.S. **1:** 39, 66; **2:** 9, 51-52, 70, 75-76; **3:** 52-53, 64, 76; **4:** 11, 13; **5:** 74; **7:** 16-17
Secretary of the Interior, U.S. **6:** 71
Secretary of the Treasury , U.S. **1:** 66; **2:** 8-13, 71; **3:** 63
Secretary of War, U.S. **1:** 66; **3:** 53
Sedition Act **2:** 43
segregation **9:** 12, 86
self-incrimination **1:** 73
Seligman, Joseph **6:** 77
Seminoles (Wars) **3:** 9, 39-44, 48, 66, 78; **5:** 23, 41
Senate, U.S. **1:** 59-62, 65; **2:** 47, 49, 80; **3:** 53, 58, 61, 66, 70, 75-76, 80; **4:** 8, 10, 13, 20, 39-40; **5:** 42, 53, 69, 74, 77-79, 84; **6:** 71 (see also Congress, U.S.)
Seneca Falls **3:** 19; **4:** 17; **7:** 41-51, 55-56; **8:** 44, 66
Senecas **9:** 87
Serra, Junípero **1:** 18
servants **6:** 22-23, 63; **7:** 63-64, 86, 77; **8:** 36, 63
Seton, Elizabeth Ann Bayley **9:** 83
Seven Years War **1:** 32-34, 68; **2:** 59; **3:** 10, 14; **4:** 78-79
Seward, William **5:** 86
sewing and sewing machines **7:** 10, 20, 67-73; **8:** 9; **9:** 11;**10:** 57
Shakers (Millennial Church) **7:** 26; **8:** 85; **9:** 55, 66, 80
Shanghai **4:** 12
Shawnees **2:** 37, 77-78, 83; **3:** 37, 48, 81; **4:** 48, 81; **9:** 87
Shays, Daniel (Rebellion) **1:** 54-55
Sheffield Scientific School **8:** 15; **9:** 15
Shelley, Mary Wollstonecraft **7:** 31
shipbuilding **6:** 58; **8:** 9; **10:** 18-19, 47-48, 56
shipping **1:** 9-10, 31, 52, 87; **2:** 29-35, 40-41, 50, 54-55, 72-74, 76, 81; **3:** 5, 10, 12, 17-19, 21-22, 26-29, 31; **4:** 12, 35-36, 38, 58-59, 68; **5:** 54-55; **6:** 5, 16, 21, 24-29, 51, 53, 72, 78-80, 87; **8:** 11, 17, 22-23; **9:** 30; **10:** 5, 14-15, 18-22, 38, 42, 45-48 (see also trade and traders)
short stories 9: 28-29, 33
Shoshones **2:** 67-68
Shreve, Henry **3:** 30-31; **8:** 17
Sickels, Frederick **8:** 9
Sierra Leone **5:** 28
Sierra Nevada Mountains **4:** 60-62, 64
Silliman, Benjamin (father) **8:** 14, 36
Silliman, Benjamin (son) **8:** 36
silver **3:** 72-73, 84; **4:** 68; **6:** 53
Sims, Thomas **5:** 45, 47
Singer, Isaac Merritt **10:** 57
Sioux **4:** 82, 84, 86
Sisters of Charity of St. Joseph **9:** 83
skilled workers **6:** 8, 11, 55-58, 60, 69, 72, 74, 76; **7:** 60, 71-72, 87; **8:** 59-61, 64; **10:** 16, 40-41, 44, 56-57
skins, animal **3:** 79; **7:** 61, 64, 72-73; **8:** 27-29, 54, 67-68; **9:** 28; **10:** 44, 56 (see also trappers and traders)
Slater, Hannah Wilkinson **7:** 85
Slater, Samuel **6:** 9, 56; **7:** 85; **10:** 40-42, 51
slaves and slavery **1:** 7-8, 10-13, 18, 22, 24, 26-27, 37, 50, 59-60, 69, 77-78, 82; **2:** 5-6; **3:** 25, 41, 48-49, 53, 58-61, 68, 78; **4:** 13-14, 24, 39, 59, 69, 78-79; **5:** 5-87; **6:** 8, 16, 24, 27, 82; **7:** 19-27, 35-36, 57, 63-65, 68, 75, 77; **8:** 28, 36, 42, 52-53, 60, 63-64, 73; **9:** 12, 47-48, 53-54, 57-58, 77-78, 85-86; **10:** 33-35, 39 (see also antislavery activities)
slaves, fugitive **2:** 87; **3:** 9, 41, 48; **5:** 22-23, 31-35, 44-49
slaves, Native-American **1:** 12, 18; **5:** 23; **9:** 87
Slave Codes **5:** 17-18, 27-28
slave revolts **3:** 68; **5:** 17-19, 21-28, 30, 50, 80-82; **9:** 38, 55
slave states **1:** 50, 60, 82; **3:** 54, 58, 81; **4:** 13, 37, 69, 78-79; **5:** 37-38, 40, 43, 56, 58-59, 70-72, 79
slave trade **1:** 10-13, 22, 31, 60; **2:** 5-6; **5:** 6-15, 23, 43, 51; **6:** 24, 27-28; **7:** 19-20; **10:** 10-11, 20
sleighs **3:** 18; **8:** 70
Sloat, John **4:** 29-30
smallpox **4:** 84; **5:** 8; **8:** 38, 41
Smith, Joseph **4:** 70-71, 73; **9:** 80
Smith, Robert **2:** 75
Smith, Samuel Francis **9:** 52
Smith, Solomon **9:** 42
Smithson, James **9:** 20
Smithsonian Institution **8:** 19, 23; **9:** 20
Snake River **2:** 64, 68; **4:** 55-56, 60
Snelling, Fort **4:** 11
soap **5:** 66; **7:** 75-76; **10:** 46
songs and songwriters **1:** 36; **2:** 84; **3:** 27; **8:** 70-71; **9:** 23, 40, 42, 46-48, 50-54, 85-86; **10:** 54
Sonoma **4:** 30
South America **1:** 12-13, 87; **3:** 9; **4:** 15, 38, 63-64; **6:** 12-13, 27, 80; **8:** 56; **9:** 30 (see also specific countries)
South and Southerners **1:** 77, 84-85; **2:** 86-87; **3:** 9, 24-25, 35, 39, 44, 58, 65, 67-68, 72, 81; **4:** 9-10, 16, 37-39, 78, 84; **5:** 5, 12-28, 30, 32-35, 37-38, 40, 43-47, 49-51, 56-59, 61, 64, 73-74, 78-80, 82-83, 86-87; **6:** 13, 33; **7:** 20, 55, 68; **8:** 56, 60, 66, 73; **9:** 7, 11-13, 15, 18, 33, 51, 77-78, 85-86; **10:** 13, 21, 29-30, 33-35, 43 (see also Old Southwest)
South Carolina **1:** 26, 64, 82, 85; **2:** 34, 38; **3:** 20, 25, 63, 66, 68-71; **5:** 25-27, 86-87; **6:** 33, 62, 75; **7:** 25; **8:** 73; **9:** 14, 36, 38, 55; **10:** 20, 66
South Dakota **10:** 65
Southern Overland Route **4:** 67, 76-77; **5:** 61-62
South Pass **4:** 41, 45-46, 48, 54, 72
Southwest **1:** 16-17, 87; **3:** 9, 44, 69, 77-85; **4:** 5, 15-16, 20-21, 76, 85; **5:** 23; **6:** 48; **8:** 27; **9:** 83, 87; **10:** 7
Southwest Territory **1:** 50
Spain **1:** 8, 10, 12, 15-18, 21-22, 41, 43, 46, 51, 53, 79, 85-87; **2:** 26, 29-30, 34-36, 59, 63, 67, 69, 73, 78, 80, 83, 87; **3:** 9, 10, 24, 41-42, 44, 48, 62, 65, 77, 81-82, 86; **4:** 69, 78-79; **5:** 23, 25, 28, 33, 56-57; **6:** 25, 75, 77-78; **9:** 87; **10:** 6
Spanish Americans **6:** 12, 85; **9:** 47, 73, 84
Spalding, Eliza Hart **9:** 81
speculation **1:** 53, 69; **3:** 13, 17, 55-57, 72-73; **4:** 17; **8:** 53, 55, 81; **10:** 19, 23, 29
speech, freedom of **1:** 72
spinning **7:** 10, 59, 67-70; **10:** 38-42, 58
spirituals **9:** 48, 85-86
Split Rock **4:** 44-45
spoils system **3:** 65
sports **8:** 73-74
Springfield **5:** 77, 84; **7:** 83; **8:** 31
stagecoaches **1:** 64; **2:** 11; **3:** 19, 22, 23, 27; **4:** 35, 39; **6:** 19; **8:** 15-16, 18, 77; **10:** 7
Staite, W. E. **8:** 37
Stamp Act **1:** 34
standardization **8:** 7, 61
Stanton, Elizabeth Cady **4:** 17; **7:** 22-23, 25-26, 28, 32, 39, 41-47, 50-51, 54-55; **8:** 62, 69, 79-80
Stanton, Henry **7:** 45, 47
"Star Spangled Banner" **2:** 84
starvation and famine **5:** 58; **6:** 14-15, 29, 43-46, 63, 65; **8:** 55; **10:** 19
statehood **1:** 49-50; **2:** 65-66; **3:** 54, 60-61; **4:** 20, 37, 59, 69, 78-79
state sovereignty **5:** 39-40, 59, 79
states' rights **1:** 37, 54, 60, 75; **2:** 6-7, 16-17, 45-46, 53, 79-80; **3:** 49-51, 57, 69-70, 74; **5:** 39
Stawianski, Fort **3:** 11
steamboats **3:** 27, 29-31; **4:** 37, 58; **6:** 23; **8:** 17, 26; **9:** 33, 45; **10:** 21
steam engines **6:** 24; **8:** 7, 9, 17-18, 25-26; **9:** 22; **10:** 37, 39, 41
steamships **6:** 16, 25, 29-32, 41, 55, 67, 79-80; **10:** 39, 43, 48
Stearns, Junius Brutus **8:** 65
steel **6:** 58; **10:** 18, 20, 25, 32, 43-44
steerage **6:** 26, 28, 31
Steinway family **9:** 52
Stephenson, George **3:** 32
Stone, John Augustus **9:** 40
Stone, Lucy **7:** 22, 38-39, 54, 58, 86; **8:** 69
Story, William **9:** 71
Stowe, Harriet Beecher **5:** 44, 48-49; **8:** 78; **9:** 32-33, 40
Strickland, William **9:** 65
strikes, labor **10:** 54-58, 60
Stuart, Gilbert **2:** 21; **9:** 67-68
Stuart, J.E.B. (Jeb) **5:** 80
Sublette, William **3:** 87; **4:** 54
Sublette's Cutoff **4:** 54
sugar **1:** 34; **2:** 10, 31; **5:** 9; **8:** 52, 53; **10:** 35
Sugar Act **1:** 34
Sully, Thomas **6:** 74
Sumter, Fort **5:** 87; **10:** 20
Superior, Lake **1:** 21; **3:** 29; **4:** 11
Supreme Court, U.S. **1:** 60-62, 67, 70-71; **2:** 32-33, 49, 53; **3:** 46, 50-51, 57, 61, 65, 74; **5:** 28, 37, 45-46, 74-76, 79; **9:** 14
surgery **8:** 9, 40-41, 47
surveyors **1:** 68; **6:** 55; **10:** 7
Sutter, John Augustus **4:** 62; **6:** 64, 66-67
Sweden **1:** 15, 24, 81, 84; **2:** 57; **9:** 59, 79
Swedish Americans **6:** 12, 19, 35, 86; **9:** 52
Sweetwater Valley (Pass) **4:** 50-51
Swiss Americans **6:** 12, 66, 85; **8:** 12; **9:** 76
Syracuse **5:** 47; **6:** 52; **7:** 43, 50; **8:** 87; **10:** 23-24

T

Talleyrand **2:** 62
Tampico **4:** 26, 32
Taney, Roger B. **3:** 74; **5:** 75-76
Taos **3:** 9, 83-84; **4:** 85
Tappan, Arthur **5:** 31, 51

taxes and tariffs **1:** 34, 54-55, 66, 77; **2:** 9-11, 13-15, 21, 51; **3:** 49, 67-70; **4:** 9, 16; **9:** 9
Taylor, Lucy Hobbs **8:** 45
Taylor, Zachary **4:** 20-22, 25-27, 31; **5:** 39-42; **10:** 68
teachers **7:** 26, 30, 50, 85; **9:** 5-13, 15, 16, 32, 47, 57
Tecumseh **2:** 77-78, 83, 86; **3:** 37; **4:** 81
telegraph **3:** 12; **4:** 9; **5:** 63; **8:** 9, 18-21
telescope **2:** 70; **8:** 22-23
temperance movement **7:** 6, 24, 28, 42; **8:** 75, 77-81
Tennessee **1:** 45, 50; **2:** 65-66; **3:** 14, 20-21, 25, 39, 46, 66, 75, 77, 79-80; **4:** 5, 15, 17; **5:** 43, 61, 86-87; **6:** 47; **9:** 14; **10:** 11, 35, 66
Tennessee Path **1:** 45; **3:** 14, 20
Tenskwatawa **2:** 80-81; **9:** 87
territorial growth, U.S. **1:** 50; **2:** 58-62, 78; **3:** 8-9; **4:** 18-20, 34; **5:** 56-57; **10:** 5-7, 10, 62-67 (see also expulsions, Native-American)
Texas **1:** 7; **2:** 57, 64; **3:** 9, 17, 39, 44, 65, 77-81; **4:** 5, 11, 13-18, 20-22, 25, 34, 37, 39, 76, 78; **5:** 33, 35, 47, 61, 87; **6:** 48, 66, 70; **9:** 82, 87; **10:** 66
Texas, Fort **4:** 21-22, 25
textile industry **6:** 56-57, 60; **7:** 67, 70-71, 73, 85; **8:** 7, 9, 83; **10:** 18-19, 38-43, 49-55, 57
Thames River **2:** 82-83
Thanksgiving **7:** 65; **8:** 50, 70-71; **9:** 53
theater **7:** 18; **9:** 25, 36-42
Thillon, Anna **9:** 60
Thoreau, Henry David **4:** 23; **8:** 87; **9:** 31-32
Thornton, William **9:** 64
three-fifths compromise **1:** 60; **3:** 58
Tillman, Juliann Jane **9:** 81
Tippecanoe **2:** 77-78; **4:** 7-8
Tlingits **7:** 68
tobacco **1:** 22-23, 31, 53; **2:** 31, 72; **3:** 24, 68; **5:** 13; **6:** 24, 69; **10:** 5, 20, 30, 35
Tom Thumb **3:** 32; **8:** 8-9, 17
Tom Thumb **9:** 45
Topeka **5:** 71
Toronto **2:** 69, 82
Town, Ithiel **9:** 65
Townshend Acts **1:** 34
trade and traders **1:** 9, 19, 21, 30-31, 34, 51-52, 60, 82-87; **2:** 6, 10, 29-37, 50, 58, 67, 69, 72-74, 76, 81-82; **3:** 6, 67-70, 73, 82, 84-87; **4:** 12, 38-41, 54-55, 81; **5:** 21; **6:** 8, 60, 74-78; **7:** 10, 12-13, 59, 65, 67, 73, 78; **8:** 11, 53, 56-57, 59-61; **10:** 5, 12, 14-15, 17-18, 21-23, 25-26, 38, 45 (see also shipping; trappers and fur traders)
Trafalgar, Cape **2:** 73
Trail of Tears **3:** 39, 46-48; **9:** 40
Transcendentalists **9:** 31, 34
transportation **4:** 35-39; **6:** 52; **8:** 15-18, 20-21, 26; **9:** 42, 44-45; **10:** 5, 29, 39, 47-48 (see also railroads; roads and trails; canals; waterways; stagecoaches; wagons; specific routes)
trappers and fur traders **1:** 19, 21, 31, 87; **2:** 37, 58, 67-69; **3:** 10, 82, 86-87; **4:** 40-41, 54-55; **6:** 9, 24, 60; **7:** 73; **8:** 54 (see also skins, animal)
Travis, William B. **3:** 79
treason **1:** 76; **2:** 71, 80
Tripoli **2:** 54-55
Troy Female Seminary **9:** 17
Trumbull, John **2:** 12; **9:** 67, 69
Truth, Sojourner **7:** 22, 26-27
Tubman, Harriet **5:** 31, 34
Tucson **5:** 61
Tully, Christopher **10:** 38

Tunis **2:** 54-55
Turner, Nat **3:** 68; **5:** 25-28, 30
Twain, Mark **9:** 33
Tyler, John **4:** 6-7, 9-11, 13; **10:** 68

U

Uncle Tom's Cabin **5:** 38, 44, 48-49; **9:** 32, 40-41
Underground Railroad **1:** 7; **5:** 1, 22, 31-35, 37, 45-46, 71; **7:** 23, 47, 53; **9:** 32
Union **1:** 63-64, 77, 84-85; **2:** 14, 46, 50, 65-66; **3:** 53, 54, 58, 60, 61, 69-70, 74, 80-81; **4:** 20, 37, 39, 59, 69, 78-79; **5:** 6-7, 11, 34, 43, 51-52, 59, 62, 70, 72-74, 76-79, 83-85; **6:** 71; **8:** 45
Union, Fort **4:** 40; **10:** 26
United Colonies **1:** 44
Utah **4:** 5, 34, 44, 55, 62, 71-75; **5:** 43, 59-60, 63; **6:** 87; **8:** 41; **10:** 66
Utes **4:** 85

V

vaccination **8:** 41
Vail, Jefferson **3:** 52
Valley Forge **1:** 40, 42, 69
Van Ambergh, Isaac **9:** 45
Van Buren, Martin **3:** 66, 71; **4:** 6, 13, 17; **5:** 40; **10:** 68
Vancouver, Fort **4:** 59
Vancouver Island **4:** 19
Vassar College **8:** 23
Vaughn, Mary C. **8:** 79
Vera Cruz **4:** 26, 32
Vermont **1:** 82; **2:** 44, 48, 65-66; **8:** 33; **9:** 14; **10:** 67
Verrazano, Giovanni da **1:** 15
Vesey, Denmark **5:** 26-27
Vice President **1:** 66; **2:** 21, 38-39, 47-48, 51-52, 70-71, 75; **3:** 63, 75-76; **4:** 6-7, 9-10; **5:** 40-41, 86; **7:** 58; **10:** 68
Vicksburg Commercial Convention **5:** 51
Virginia **1:** 22-23, 26, 42, 51, 55, 63-64, 68-71, 82, 84-85; **2:** 38, 45-47, 50, 52, 76; **3:** 20, 23, 25, 34, 51-53, 68-69, 80; **4:** 6-10; **5:** 6-7, 13, 17-18, 23, 25-27, 34, 40, 47, 80-82, 87; **6:** 62; **7:** 19; **8:** 29; **9:** 13, 36, 63-64, 75, 13, 67
Virginia Minstrels **9:** 41-42
Virginia Resolution **2:** 45-46
Virginia, University of **9:** 63

W

Wabash River **2:** 37
wages **7:** 32, 42, 60, 64, 87; **9:** 10-11; **10:** 49, 53-57, 60
wagons **3:** 5, 12, 14, 18-20, 22-23, 82, 84; **4:** 41, 44-57, 61, 63, 70, 72-73, 81; **5:** 38; **6:** 75, 77; **7:** 69; **8:** 24 (see also transportation; roads and trails; handcarts)
Wales **1:** 25, 81; **6:** 7
Walker, David **5:** 30
Walker, Mary **8:** 69
Walker, William **5:** 56-57
Wallsmith, Christopher **6:** 72
Walter, Thomas Ustick **9:** 65
Waltham **10:** 42, 52-55
Wanghia, Treaty of **4:** 12
War Hawks **2:** 79-80
War of 1812 **2:** 49, 55-57, 69, 76-86; **3:** 5-6, 24-25, 34-35, 39, 52, 55, 63-64, 66; **4:** 8; **5:** 41; **6:** 5, 54, 60; **7:** 17; **8:** 72; **9:** 42; **10:** 35, 47

Warren, Mercy Otis **7:** 9; **9:** 27
washing and cleaning **7:** 24, 60, 62-63, 70-77; **8:** 67; **9:** 17
Washington (state) **3:** 86; **4:** 19, 59, 79, 83, 87; **10:** 66-67
Washington, D.C. **2:** 10, 44, 47, 83-84; **3:** 25, 65, 72; **4:** 7, 31, 39; **5:** 14, 43, 52, 63-64, 85; **6:** 55, 85; **7:** 12, 16-18; **8:** 19-20, 34, 74; **9:** 37, 39, 62-64; **10:** 62
Washington, Fort **6:** 63; **7:** 11
Washington, George **1:** 7, 27, 32-33, 35, 41, 55-58, 61, 65-69; **2:** 7, 14-15, 19, 21-23, 26-30, 37-39, 56; **3:** 53, 74; **5:** 5, 50, 77; **6:** 73-74; **7:** 8, 10, 14-15; **8:** 29, 38, 63, 65; **9:** 14, 64, 68; **10:** 68
Washington, Martha **7:** 10, 14-15; **8:** 63, 65
Washington Monument **5:** 52; **9:** 64-65
water **7:** 62, 74-77; **8:** 7, 9, 24-25, 28, 34, 39; **9:** 64; **10:** 28, 33, 36-38, 41
waterways **1:** 19, 83; **2:** 10; **3:** 18-19, 56; **4:** 35-36; **6:** 16, 47; **8:** 15-17, 26; **9:** 42, 44; **10:** 12, 25, 37 (see also canals; specific canals and rivers)
Watt, James **8:** 25; **10:** 39
Waugh, Samuel B. **6:** 53
Wayne, Anthony **2:** 37
weaving **10:** 59, 67-70; **8:** 8-9; **10:** 38-39, 42, 55-56
Webster, Daniel **3:** 70, 75; **4:** 9, 23; **9:** 14
Webster, Noah **9:** 10, 14
Webster-Ashburton Treaty **3:** 8; **4:** 9, 11
Weld, Theodore **5:** 31
Wells, Horace **8:** 41
Welsh Americans **6:** 7, 17, 54, 57-58
Wesley, John **9:** 77
West, Benjamin **1:** 24; **9:** 67-68
West and Westerners **2:** 65-69, 71, 73; **3:** 27, 63-64, 72, 86-87; **4:** 29, 38-87; **5:** 60-63, 67-70; **6:** 6, 33-34, 48, 52-53, 66, 81-83; **7:** 34, 52, 55, 73; **9:** 23, 69-70, 78; **10:** 11, 21-22, 26, 30, 39
West Coast: See Pacific coast
Western Female Institute **9:** 16
West Indies **1:** 31, 51; **2:** 12, 79; **8:** 11
Weston, Edward Payson **8:** 74
West Point **2:** 57; **3:** 7; **9:** 15; **10:** 16
West Virginia **3:** 20, 23; **5:** 80; **10:** 67
whaling **3:** 11; **4:** 38; **8:** 11, 35; **9:** 30, 47; **10:** 5, 45-46
Whampoa **1:** 52
Wheelock, Eleazar **9:** 14
Whigs **3:** 75-76; **4:** 6, 8-10, 13, 15-16, 22-23; **5:** 37, 39, 41, 52-53, 59, 64, 67-68, 74, 84, 86; **10:** 68
Whipple, Squire **8:** 33
Whiskey Rebellion **1:** 66; **2:** 13-15, 21; **8:** 81
Whistler, James Abbott **9:** 48
White, Hugh **3:** 75
White Americans **1:** 6-8, 81; **3:** 68; **5:** 18, 44, 80; **6:** 7, 83; **7:** 20, 23; **8:** 46-47, 62, 73; **9:** 10-13, 18, 41, 55, 86; **10:** 10, 62-67
White House **2:** 38, 48, 83-84; **3:** 52, 65; **4:** 7; **5:** 63, 73; **7:** 12, 15-18; **9:** 63-64
Whitman, Marcus **3:** 86
Whitman, Narcissa **3:** 86; **9:** 81
Whitman, Walt **9:** 35
Whitney, Eli **3:** 24; **5:** 13; **8:** 7, 61; **10:** 33-34, 39, 44
Whittier, John Greenleaf **9:** 34
Whittredge, Worthington **9:** 70
Wilberforce College **9:** 18
Wild, John Casper **4:** 11
Wilderness Road **1:** 29, 45; **3:** 13, 14, 20-21

Willamette River **4:** 42, 56-58
Willard, Emma Hart **9:** 17
William and Mary, College of **2:** 52; **4:** 10; **9:** 13
Williams, Roger **1:** 85
Williamsburg **9:** 13, 36
Wilmington **1:** 24; **6:** 86
Wilmot, David (Proviso) **4:** 24
windmills **8:** 24-26
Winnebagos **3:** 37
Winner, Septimus **9:** 53
Winnipesaukee, Lake **8:** 74
Wisconsin **1:** 49; **3:** 17-18, 38; **4:** 37, 78; **5:** 46, 75; **6:** 54, 58, 61, 70, 72, 87; **8:** 26; **9:** 10, 76; **10:** 5, 67
Wise, Isaac Meyer **9:** 84
Wollstonecraft, Mary **7:** 29-32
Woman's Rights Convention, Seneca Falls **4:** 17; **7:** 23, 41-51; **8:** 68
women **1:** 58, 71; **3:** 14, 37-38, 86; **5:** 31; **6:** 11, 15, 23, 74; **7:** 5-87; **8:** 40; **9:** 6, 81; **10:** 52-55, 57
women, single **7:** 5, 33, 35, 38, 59
women, votes for **7:** 5, 7, 21, 45-47, 54, 56; **8:** 80
women's rights **1:** 78; **4:** 17; **5:** 19, 20; **7:** 9, 12-13, 20-58, 61, 84-87; **8:** 44, 75, 79-81; **9:** 24, 31
women's rights conventions, national **7:** 27-28, 50, 52-54, 57
Wood, Jethro **10:** 31-21
wood and woodworking **1:** 53; **4:** 58-59, 63; **5:** 51; **6:** 24, 32, 41, 60, 72, 87; **8:** 27-30, 37, 59-60; **10:** 20, 23, 31, 44
Woodworth, Samuel **9:** 23
wool **1:** 53; **7:** 67-69; **8:** 66; **10:** 30, 42, 44
Worcester **7:** 28, 54-55
Worcester v. Georgia **3:** 46
working bee **7:** 10, 71; **8:** 37, 58
working conditions **5:** 9, 18; **7:** 22, 84; **8:** 75; **9:** 30, 32; **10:** 49, 50-58, 60 (see also slaves and slavery; mills and factories; child labor)
Wounded Knee Massacre **4:** 86
Wright, Martha **7:** 44
writers and writing **2:** 18; **6:** 71; **7:** 9, 11, 19, 23, 30-31, 38, 57-58, 65-66, 85; **9:** 6, 8, 12, 25 (see also literature)
Wyandots **3:** 37
Wyeth, Nathaniel **3:** 87; **4:** 55
Wyoming **2:** 59; **4:** 34, 41, 44, 50, 74, 86; **10:** 66-67

X

XYZ Affair **2:** 41

Y

Yale College (University) **8:** 14, 36, 74; **9:** 13, 15-16
yellow fever **8:** 38-39, 44
Yellowstone **2:** 59; **3:** 31; **10:** 26
York **2:** 69, 82
Yorktown **1:** 42, 51, 69
Young Men's Christian Association **8:** 76
Young, Brigham **4:** 71-75

Z

Zane's Trace **3:** 20-21
Ziegler, David **6:** 63

96